Praise f

MW01152347

A major strength is the nature of the journey through which the author takes the reader that builds passion and a 'can do' spirit along the path. This should be required reading for ALL who participate in the education profession and highly encouraged for anyone interested in the future of our world.

—Judith A. Rogers, Education Consultant
Associates for Educational Success
Tucson, Arizona

If you've stayed awake at night wondering how to create innovative education to meet the learning needs of today's students and their families, worry no more! The author presents a broad range of current instructional trends in a practical, engaging way with useful questions for further thought.

—Virginia E. Kelsen, Executive Director, Career Readiness
Chaffey Joint Union High School District
Ontario, California

All Together Now *provides rich examples of innovative practices taking place in innovative schools and districts. Educators looking to transform student learning will gain insight on how to implement ideas into the classroom.*

—Winston Sakurai, Upper School Principal
Hanalani Schools
Mililani, Hawaii

There have been many good books on the case for 21st century learning and schools, but only a rare handful on how to engage your stakeholders and community to bring that transformation to your own school or district. Fortunately, education writer and consultant Suzie Boss takes up that challenge and shares the stories of real-world school transformers and school transformations from around the world.

—Bob Pearlman, 21st Century School and District Consultant
Tucson, Arizona

I love Suzie's new book because it tackles the challenge of how to rally educators, parents, community members, and students around new visions of learning and teaching. Like her previous books, this one is rooted in the concrete strategies and techniques that numerous schools are using to create deeper, more engaging—and, yes, more successful—learning environments for children. If you're a transformational educator or policymaker who is looking for models and exemplars, use this book to learn from some of the most interesting, visionary schools in the world and inspire your own change processes.

—Dr. Scott McLeod, Associate Professor of Educational Leadership
Founding Director of CASTLE; University of Colorado
Denver, Colorado

School innovation is a subject that should concern all of us—students, educators, parents, community members. Suzie Boss has created a wonderful guide for all of us to think deeply, reflect critically, and act decisively to make schools better for all of us who need them.

—Chris Lehmann, Founding Principal and Author of *Building School 2.0*
Science Leadership Academy
Philadelphia, Pennsylvania 19103

You won't find a better guide to the numerous and wide-ranging school improvement strategies out there than in All Together Now!

—Larry Ferlazzo, educator, author, and *Education Week* teacher advice columnist
Luther Burbank High School
Sacramento, California

This is a clear blueprint for real change in modern schools. A variety of frameworks including PBL, design thinking, making, student leadership, and parent empowerment are illustrated with examples from real schools and stellar advice from educators. Educators on the road to remaking their schools into better learning spaces should take this book with them on the journey.

—Sylvia Martinez, co-author of *Invent To Learn: Making, Tinkering, and Engineering in the Classroom*

In All Together Now, *Suzie Boss brings clarity and real-world examples for those seeking inspiration and solutions to build K-12 schools much needed for the twenty-first century. This book puts your finger on the pulse of the best examples of schools that help our students gain the skills to meet future challenges and opportunities.*

—Cindy Johanson, Executive Director
Edutopia

Boss surveys the bewildering landscape of school initiatives and helps the reader identify key features they can adopt and adapt to improve their community's schools. She illuminates complex ideas with concrete examples from exemplary schools in the U.S. and abroad. This is a school transformation guide suitable for all stakeholders.

—David Ross, CEO
Partnership for 21st Century Learning

All Together Now *should be required reading for school, district, and community leaders as well as aspiring leaders in graduate school programs. Suzie Boss uses her amazing story telling and journalistic talents to highlight the communities, districts, schools, and programs that are pointing the way for the future of learning. Boss uses straightforward language to lay out the challenges and potential solutions for educator and community leaders to work together toward preparing students for success in the 21st century workplace and society.* All Together Now *is rich with suggested resources for those who are inspired to act. Facts, stories, and resources—this book is a one stop inspirational tool for education and community leaders.*

—Bob Lenz, Executive Director
Buck Institute for Education
Novato, California

ALL Together NOW

How to Engage Your Stakeholders in Reimagining School

SUZIE BOSS

Foreword by Ken Kay

CORWIN
A SAGE Publishing Company

A SAGE Publishing Company

FOR INFORMATION:

Corwin

A SAGE Company

2455 Teller Road

Thousand Oaks, California 91320

(800) 233-9936

www.corwin.com

SAGE Publications Ltd.

1 Oliver's Yard

55 City Road

London EC1Y 1SP

United Kingdom

SAGE Publications India Pvt. Ltd.

B 1/I 1 Mohan Cooperative Industrial Area

Mathura Road, New Delhi 110 044

India

SAGE Publications Asia-Pacific Pte. Ltd.

3 Church Street

#10-04 Samsung Hub

Singapore 049483

Executive Editor: Arnis Burvikovs

Senior Associate Editor: Desirée A. Bartlett

Editorial Assistant: Kaitlyn Irwin

Production Editor: Veronica Stapleton Hooper

Copy Editor: Amy Hanquist Harris

Typesetter: Hurix Systems Pvt. Ltd.

Proofreader: Dennis W. Webb

Indexer: Sheila Bodell

Cover Designer: Anupama Krishnan

Marketing Manager: Anna Mesick

Printed in the United States of America

Library of Congress Cataloging-in-Publication Data

Names: Boss, Suzie, author.

Title: All together now : how to engage your stakeholders in reimagining school / Suzie Boss ; foreword by Ken Kay.

Description: Thousand Oaks, California : Corwin, [2017] | Includes bibliographical references and index.

Identifiers: LCCN 2016059351 | ISBN 9781506350127 (pbk. : alk. paper)

Subjects: LCSH: School improvement programs.

Classification: LCC LB2822.8 .B65 2017 | DDC 371.2/07–dc23 LC record available at https://lccn .loc.gov/2016059351

This book is printed on acid-free paper.

Certified Sourcing
www.sfiprogram.org
SFI-00453

17 18 19 20 21 10 9 8 7 6 5 4 3 2 1

Contents

All the online resources and links mentioned in the book are available for readers to access at **www.corwin.com/alltogethernow**.

Foreword

The last 15 years of education policy and debate in the United States have failed to transform our education system. We find ourselves in essentially the same corner we found ourselves at the dawn of the 21st century, but drawn more urgently than ever toward a new paradigm. At this juncture, we must empower local communities, school boards, and superintendents to reenergize and refocus our schools and districts for the 21st century. Federal and state policy makers have been wracked by steep ideological divisions, confused by differing visions of the purpose of education, and obsessed with punitive accountability measures and outdated standards. It now falls on local education leaders and their stakeholders to lead our nation's schools beyond our country's politicized and systematic intransigence.

The good news is that there are dozens of leaders and communities ready for this challenge. For the last six years, I have had the privilege to advise and to learn from these leaders as the CEO of EdLeader21. Our professional learning community comprises education leaders committed to transforming their schools and districts so their students are truly ready for the challenges of 21st century life, citizenship, and work. Our collaboration has led me to a very optimistic but clear-eyed view of what can happen if we give our local education leaders and their communities the flexibility and support they need to move education transformation forward.

The most successful leaders of this groundbreaking work demonstrate a variety of shared commitments. They are devoted to disrupting the traditional education model, to engaging their communities in dialogue, and to changing classroom pedagogy and practice so that every student actually develops the necessary skills to be successful in the 21st century. When I address education transformation, I often ask who would make the better employee, family member, and citizen: "Student A" or "Student B"?

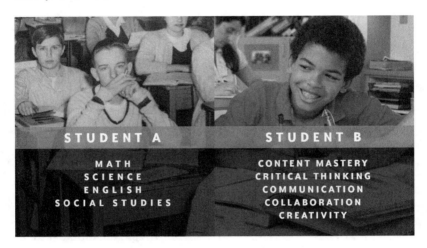

Invariably, school stakeholders select Student B—then wonder, after endless years of fierce debate and countless millions of dollars invested, how we can still be stuck in an education system devoted almost exclusively to Student A.

Rejecting decades of myopic education debate, policy, and practice, the dynamic education leaders in our PLC have had the courage and conviction to rally their schools and districts around the growth of Student B. They often articulate the proficiencies of Student B in a "Profile of a 21st Century Graduate" (see www.profileofagraduate .org), then engage their stakeholders in robust and sustained dialogue about it. These leaders realize that in order for transformation to be successful, it needs to be rooted in a vision that stakeholders not only understand but also have been given the opportunity to shape and support.

Suzie Boss's work in *All Together Now: How to Engage Your Stakeholders in Reimagining School* provides educators with the first comprehensive guide to engaging each of their school community's key constituencies—students and their families, teachers and principals, school board, youth groups, and business leaders—in dialogue about 21st century education transformation. The book not only suggests helpful strategies to approach each group but also provides impactful ways to frame and sustain dialogue with them. This "stakeholder guide" will be invaluable to those education leaders who are undertaking the transformation dialogue with their communities and will be hailed as such for years to come.

At the end of the day, all of our schools' stakeholders recognize, or can be helped to recognize, the urgency of retooling our schools and districts. They must support the development of young people who can engage with their communities to identify and address their most vexing problems. They must help students collaborate across difference to harness a diversity of strengths and perspectives. They must help students learn to reinvent themselves, their institutions, their products, and their communities to serve the needs of a changing world. These skills will provide young adults with economic opportunity and empower them to respond to a vast array of 21st century challenges in their society, their workplace, and their world. Simply put, those who develop these skills will be successful in the coming decades; those who don't will not.

This reality applies globally. Over the last few years, I have had the privilege to visit Finland, Thailand, and Singapore and to participate in a global conference on 21st century education hosted by Fernando Reimers at Harvard. In these international contexts, my global colleagues confirmed that there is much attention being paid to the development of transformative 21st century educational systems outside the United States. And they have confirmed how important vision, messaging, and community engagement are to the success of these efforts in their countries.

Around the globe, students need to learn to adapt and to change. They are depending on our schools to do the same. More and more local education leaders and their communities are seizing the freedom, agency, and courage to exercise these skills themselves; together, they will usher in the next great era of education. This crucial book will be indispensable to supporting their efforts.

Ken Kay

Ken Kay was the founding president of The Partnership for 21st Century Skills in 2002. He now serves as CEO of EdLeader21, a professional learning community of leaders dedicated to implementing 21st century education. He is the coauthor of *The Leader's Guide to 21st Century Education: 7 Steps for Schools and Districts*.

Preface

Earlier in my career, I worked for an educational research lab. Much of our work focused on putting good ideas into practice to improve academic results in high-poverty communities. The goal wasn't so much adopting break-the-mold models of education as it was catching up with schools that did better by traditional measures. My work often involved translating educational research for lay audiences. As I listened for questions from parents and other community members, I heard a common concern: *How is this going to be better for our kids?*

A couple decades later, a new call for school transformation is once again raising questions from stakeholders. I'm at a different point in my career now as an education writer and consultant focusing on project-based learning and innovation. I have been fortunate to work with schools of all descriptions, both across the United States and internationally, that are retooling to be more relevant for today's learners. I hear challenging conversations unfolding in a wide range of settings, including public school districts and charters, independent schools, and international schools. Across diverse contexts, there's little disagreement that schools based on last century's model *must* change. Blue-ribbon panels, best-selling authors, and impassioned keynote speakers have made a convincing case: if we want today's students to be better equipped to tackle the complex challenges ahead, we must update or reinvent how schools help them learn.

Yet hard questions remain when it comes to moving forward: How fast, how far should changes go? Which traditions and instructional strategies are worth preserving? How can we ensure that new approaches, including the use of digital tools, will lead to better learning outcomes? How can learning spaces be redesigned to support reimagined instructional goals? How will we avoid burnout or indifference among teachers who have seen previous initiatives come and go? And, of course, the essential question we must ask of any school change: *How is this going to be better for our kids?*

One more question is making the rounds, too, in communities that are taking real action to reinvent education. Today's parents and community partners don't just want to know how or why education is changing. They also want to know, *How can we help?* As schools look beyond the classroom to create real-world learning opportunities for their students, new avenues are opening for family and community participation. Students themselves are speaking up about how, when, and where they learn best.

That's good news. At a time of rapid global change and an explosion of information, schools can't expect to find all the answers within their own campuses. Instead, many schools are turning outward, engaging everyone in their communities—students, teachers, parents, school boards, business leaders, and other partners—to dream together about the future of learning and then work together to make it happen.

AUDIENCE

This book is for anyone who is concerned about the future of K–12 education, committed to engaging students in more meaningful learning, and convinced that school change will require collaborative effort by stakeholders who may not have a track record of working together. The primary audience includes the diverse community of educators who focus every day on serving their students' best interests. This includes school and district leaders, teachers and instructional coaches, technology and media specialists, school governance boards and policy makers. Readers are also likely to include parents and other allies for school change from the business community, nonprofits, philanthropic sector, and school architects and others in the design field. Additionally, the book offers practical ideas that should be useful for networks and affinity groups already pursuing initiatives such as project-based learning, design thinking, makerspaces, and other efforts to promote more meaningful, student-driven instruction.

By now, nearly two decades into the 21st century, we can look to a substantial body of literature to understand why last century's model of schooling fails to adequately equip students for careers and citizenship in our fast-changing world. That's why, in the pages ahead, readers should not expect to find another treatise on the need for school change. Instead, this book is about what happens next, once your community decides that it's time to stop debating and start working together to prepare your students for the challenges and opportunities ahead.

APPROACH AND ORGANIZATION

Like instructional practices that are grounded in inquiry, this book prompts readers to make their own meaning by considering a series of questions. Abundant examples and case studies from the front-lines of school change provide inspiration and ideas you can adopt or adapt for your context. Discussion prompts are included to promote and provoke conversations—both inside and outside school—with everyone who has a stake in student success (including students themselves). Working together, through collaborative inquiry and hard conversations, you will arrive at your best answers for how schools should adapt for your context and your children.

The book is organized to guide you through a four-part process for engaging stakeholders in school change.

Part I: The Why focuses on motivation. What's the shared "why" that is motivating community members to tackle the hard work of school change? The first chapter briefly recaps global efforts to transform education, acknowledges barriers to change, and asks readers to evaluate their community's readiness for disruption. Chapter 2 introduces stakeholder engagement strategies that communities have used to effectively "engage the willing" in rethinking school.

Part II: The How is about moving from shared vision to new reality by keeping everyone engaged. Chapter 3 describes grassroots visioning processes that invite the perspectives of diverse stakeholders, from within schools and from the broader community. Chapters 4 through 7 focus on strategies to engage specific stakeholder groups critical to any change initiative, including teachers, students, families, and other community allies.

Part III: The What-ifs focuses on maintaining momentum and overcoming resistance. Chapter 8 guides readers to start with the end in mind and to clearly define the goals of change efforts and the indicators of progress. To anticipate roadblocks and overcome pushback, readers consider how they will respond to common concerns ("yeah, buts" and "what-ifs") that can slow or derail initiatives. Troubleshooting strategies help leaders become more effective change managers.

Part IV: The Future Story highlights the power of storytelling to sustain change and build optimism for future efforts. Chapter 9 explains how sharing stories of school transformation helps communities celebrate early wins and stay committed to long-term change. Chapter 10 revisits the big questions asked throughout the book and encourages readers to plan their next steps.

OUTCOMES

What should readers know and be able to do by the end of the book? Outcomes will no doubt vary, depending on your starting point and readiness for disruption. In broad strokes, however, readers can expect to come away with these things:

- Greater clarity about their community's readiness for school change
- Creative ways to identify diverse and perhaps underrepresented stakeholder groups and engage them as school change partners (including nontraditional roles for parents that leverage their talents and interests)
- Practical ideas to amplify student voice in learning and leadership
- Strategies for overcoming resistance to change and avoiding initiative fatigue
- Suggestions for making deliberate use of digital tools and storytelling to shape the narrative about education in your community
- Permission to dream big about the future of teaching and learning

SPECIAL FEATURES

Throughout the book, special features are included to help guide your inquiry:

Worth Asking: Each chapter includes questions intended to prompt individual reflection or spark group discussions about featured case studies and other examples of creative community outreach. Share your responses with a broader community on Twitter by adding the hashtag #alltogethernow.

Crib Sheet: Short, jargon-free summaries of key terms are included to ensure that everyone is talking the same language about current trends in education. Along with brief definitions, you'll find links for additional resources and hashtags to connect with communities of practice.

Try This: Watch for practical ideas that are ready to borrow or adapt. Try This suggestions challenge readers to apply specific activities or outreach strategies that other schools have found to be beneficial.

Web Resources: All the online resources and links mentioned in the book will be available for readers to access at www.corwin.com/alltogethernow.

How to Use This Book

This book will ask you to wrestle with big questions about where education is heading. There is no answer key, although there are abundant examples and case studies to inspire your thinking. This emphasis on inquiry shouldn't be surprising, given my longtime advocacy of project-based learning and other approaches that emphasize open-ended questions as springboards for deep and meaningful learning. Finding the right answers for your community will depend on your local context and your prior experiences. Some readers will likely be deep into visioning work with their communities. Others may be just beginning to consider whether their schools are overdue for an update to meet the needs of today's learners.

The focus on stakeholder engagement makes the book ideally suited to read and discuss with others. Case studies and questions throughout the book are included to promote and provoke conversation. Perhaps those conversations will be a first step toward deeper community engagement. This might happen informally or in more structured ways, such as in a book group or professional learning community. To that end, you will find a discussion guide in Appendix B.

A Note on the Stories and Sources

The book includes extensive examples and case studies from schools and communities in diverse settings, both in the United States and internationally. Several such stories are woven throughout the book, illustrating how innovative schools and communities have advanced their own journeys to create new learning opportunities for students. Unless otherwise indicated, stories in the coming chapters were shared by sources personally interviewed by the author. They have granted permission to be quoted in the book.

Acknowledgments

Many people contributed stories and suggestions to bring this book to life.

I would like to thank the team at Corwin for helping me think through the message I wanted to share and the audience I hoped to reach. Thanks especially to Arnis Burvikovs and Desirée A. Bartlett for editorial advice that helped to shape the book. Thanks, too, to Amy Harris for her careful copyediting and to Kaitlyn Irwin to attending to myriad publishing details.

I am honored that Ken Kay, CEO of EdLeader21 and a longtime advocate of 21st century teaching and learning, agreed to share his perspective by contributing the Foreword.

Fittingly for a book titled *All Together Now*, stakeholders from a variety of contexts shared insights about the challenges facing schools and the courage required to rethink education. Among those who offered their wisdom about schools around the world were leadership expert Scott McLeod, Shabbi Luthra, and Scot Hoffman of the American School of Bombay, global school planner Frank Locker, and Brett Jacobson from Mount Vernon Presbyterian School. Silvia Tolisano, connected-learning expert, contributed important ideas about storytelling as a vehicle for improving our practice as educators.

I was inspired by the creativity and collaboration to reinvent learning across the Remake Learning network in Pittsburgh, Pennsylvania. Thanks especially to Gregg Behr of the Grable Foundation, Cathy Lewis Long of the Sprout Fund, Superintendent Bart Rocco of Elizabeth Forward School District, and Shaun Tomaszewski from Pittsburgh Public Schools.

In Chesterfield County Schools, Virginia, former Superintendent Marcus Newsome and Chief Academic Officer Donna Dalton generously took time to reflect on the process that has engaged stakeholders in school change. The team at Iowa BIG shared its powerful story about rethinking high school. Thanks to Dr. Trace Pickering and Troy Miller for your insights.

I had the opportunity to deepen my understanding of how architects and educators are collaborating to reimagine schools by attending the National Summit on School Design. Thanks to the American Architectural Foundation (AAF) for hosting, and thanks to Ron Bogle, AAF CEO and president, for follow-up conversations about the Design for Learning initiative.

As an example of school–community partnerships, I have followed with interest the development of the EF Glocal Challenge in Cambridge, Massachusetts. Thanks to Shawna Sullivan Marino from EF Education First and Jennifer Lawrence with the city of Cambridge Community Development Department for thinking through their strategies for building an effective program that enables students to take on real-world challenges.

I greatly appreciate the students who contributed insights and perspectives. Zak Malamad and Andrew Brennen from #stuvoice were particularly helpful in bringing student voice into the conversation. And Sylvia Martinez helped me appreciate that student voice involves more than listening; it's about student action. Thanks for the useful feedback.

Finally, I'd like to acknowledge the many others who are hard at work on making school more meaningful and engaging in communities across the United States and around the world. I hope you continue to share your stories, setbacks, and strategies so that others can learn from your experiences.

Publisher's Acknowledgments

Corwin gratefully acknowledges the contributions of the following reviewers:

Virginia E. Kelsen, Executive Director, Career Readiness
Chaffey Joint Union High School District
Ontario, California

Renee Peoples, Instructional Coach
West Elementary School
Bryson City, North Carolina

Judith A. Rogers, Education Consultant
Associates for Educational Success
Tucson, Arizona

Winston Sakurai, Upper School Principal
Hanalani Schools
Mililani, Hawaii

About the Author

Suzie Boss is a writer and educational consultant who focuses on the power of teaching and learning to improve lives and transform communities. She is the author of several popular books for educators, including *Bringing Innovation to School, Reinventing Project-Based Learning* (coauthored with Jane Krauss), and *Setting the Standard for Project Based Learning* (coauthored with John Larmer and John Mergendoller). She is a regular contributor to *Edutopia* and the *Stanford Social Innovation Review* in addition to being a member of the Buck Institute for Education National Faculty. She is collaborating with award-winning global educator Stephen Ritz on *The Power of a Plant*, which tells his inspiring story of creating green classrooms and healthier outcomes for children and communities across New York's South Bronx and around the world.

Inspired by teachers who push the boundaries of the traditional classroom, Suzie consults with schools internationally that are ready to shift away from tests and textbooks and engage students in real-world problem solving. She has helped project-based learning take hold at schools in India, Europe, Mexico, and South America, as well as all over the United States. Beyond the regular school day, she has developed programs that teach youth and adults how to improve their communities with innovative, sustainable solutions.

Her wide-ranging interests in education were shaped by several years as a writer, editor, and field researcher for the Northwest

Regional Educational Laboratory (now Education Northwest) and earlier experiences as a community college instructor and journalist. She lives in Portland, Oregon, where she enjoys exploring the outdoors, playing tennis, and spending time with her husband and two grown sons.

PART I

The Why

What's the shared "why" that is motivating your community members to tackle the hard work of school change? How ready is your community for the disruption that is certain to accompany any school change initiative? To help diverse stakeholders have productive conversations about these questions, this section begins with a short recap of global efforts to transform education for 21st century learners. How will you engage a coalition of the willing to rethink school for your community?

CHAPTER 1

Are we ready for disruption?

> "We owe it to all of the people—students, teachers, parents—
> who bring the best of themselves to the flawed systems of
> school every day to make those systems better tomorrow than
> they are today. But we also owe it to those people to make
> that evolution as painless as possible, so that the upheaval and
> disruption do not mean the loss of dignity and learning and
> care for the people who inhabit our schools."
> —Chris Lehmann and Zac Chase, *Building
> School 2.0,* 2015, p. 32

In this chapter, as we prepare to consider strategies to engage the
wider community in school change, let's first review key arguments for why change is necessary for our students' success. Building common understanding among stakeholders—who likely bring different expectations, experiences, and perspectives about school—will lead to more productive discussions about potentially unfamiliar pedagogies and global education trends. The chapter concludes with a look at catalysts that are accelerating school change—any one of which may be the spark for disruption in your community.

TRENDS FOR TRANSFORMATION

Ready or not, education is changing. The trends that are rapidly reshaping our schools go by many names—blended learning, personalized learning, project-based learning, deeper learning, maker education, connected learning, design thinking, and more. Each approach comes with its own champions, teaching practices, and even hashtags.

3

These 21st century pedagogies are more alike than different. Although distinctive, each approach promises to create opportunities for students to develop the capacities they need to thrive in a fast-changing world. They all incorporate digital tools for connecting and creating, extending learning from the classroom into the wider world. They all challenge students to take a more active role in their own learning and to solve problems in their own communities—and perhaps beyond. In different ways, each approach has the potential to disrupt traditional education. See Crib Sheet 101 for a short definition of the instructional practices mentioned previously. These practices will be discussed in many of the case studies to come.

CRIB SHEET 101

Pedagogies and Practices for Transformative Teaching and Learning

In an effort to transform education to better meet the needs of today's learners, schools are adopting a wide range of instructional strategies and classroom practices that differ in significant ways from traditional teacher-directed, textbook-based schooling. In coming chapters, you will hear educators refer to the following approaches as part of their strategies for school change. No single idea offers a perfect solution. Many schools mix and match these approaches to meet the needs of diverse learners.

It's only natural for stakeholders to compare emerging practices with their own experience of school. In different ways, the following approaches challenge the familiar model of education—the teacher in charge at the front of the room, students seated in rows, compliance and order valued over creativity and teamwork. Not only is that model familiar, but it may have worked perfectly well for many stakeholders. Teachers, parents, and other community members have good reason to question why the "old school" model that they know and trust is being replaced by something unfamiliar.

Avoiding jargon and using common definitions to discuss new ideas will help stakeholders have more productive discussions about potentially unfamiliar pedagogies. In the following paragraphs, you'll find brief definitions of key terms to help you build shared understanding. You will hear these terms throughout the coming chapters as communities in different contexts consider ideas for school transformation. Suggestions for additional resources to explore and a Twitter hashtag to connect with a community of practice are included for each practice or approach.

Blended learning. Students engage in a combination of online and face-to-face learning, allowing them to make choices about the pace, location, and timing of their learning experiences. To learn more, visit the Christensen Institute, which describes four models of blended learning (www.tinyurl.com/zrpyfot). Follow #blendedlearning.

Connected learning. Leveraging digital tools and peer-to-peer learning, connected learning is socially connected, interest-driven, and academically oriented, according to the Connected Learning Research Network (clrn.dmlhub.net). Connected learning occurs across the lifespan and leads naturally to network building (such as the personal learning networks that many educators rely on for personalized professional learning). To learn more:, visit Educator Innovator, a resource from the National Writing Project (www.educatorinnovator.org), or follow research discussions at www.clrn.dmlhub.net. Follow #connectedlearning.

Deeper learning. Students across the 500 diverse schools that are part of the Deeper Learning Network develop six core competences: master core academic content, think critically and solve complex problems, work collaboratively, communicate effectively, learn how to learn, and develop academic mindsets. Wall-to-wall, project-based learning is also a common feature of these schools, which include public district schools and charters. To learn more:, visit www.deeperlearning4all.org or follow #deeperlearning.

Design thinking. This open-ended problem-solving process that has wide use in commercial product design and social innovation is rapidly migrating to the classroom. Design thinking typically starts by identifying user needs through empathy-building experiences before moving to defining, ideating, prototyping, and refining results based on feedback. The process is iterative rather than linear, producing multiple drafts and prototypes en route to innovation. To learn more, visit the d.school Institute of Design at Stanford University (dschool.stanford.edu) or download a free toolkit, *Design Thinking for Educators* (www.designthinkingforeducators.com/toolkit). Follow #designthinking.

4Cs. The 4Cs, advocated by the Partnership for 21st Century Learning, EdLeader21, and others, is a shorthand for describing these four competencies that are considered essential for life and work in the 21st century: communication, collaboration, critical thinking, and creativity. To learn more, visit P21 (www.p21.0rg). Follow #4Cs.

Flipped learning. A modification of blended learning, flipped learning replaces traditional classroom lectures with video recordings, which students typically view as homework. To learn more, visit the Flipped Learning Global Initiative (www.flglobal.org) launched by flipped-learning pioneer and evangelist Jon Bergman. Follow #flippedlearning.

Genius Hour. Modeled on an idea from Google and other companies to free up 20 percent of employees' time for self-directed research projects, Genius Hour creates time and space within the school week for students to pursue questions that pique their curiosity. To learn more, study the principles of Genius Hour on *TeachThought* (www.tinyurl.com/pavknc2). Follow #geniushour.

Global education. In an increasingly interconnected world, students develop global competence by investigating issues of global importance, recognizing multiple perspectives, communicating their views, and taking action. To learn more, read *Educating for Global Competence* (Boix Mansilla & Jackson, 2011), published by the Council of Chief School Officers and the Asia Society (free download available at asiasociety. org/files/book-globalcompetence.pdf), or *Empowering Global Citizens: A World Course* (Reimers, Chopra, Chung, Higdon, & O'Donnell, 2016). Take part in global education events and find more resources at the Global Education Conference Network (www.globaleducationconference.com). Follow #globaled.

Maker education. Grounded in the philosophy of learning by doing, maker education provides students with access to tools and the time to solve problems that interest them. To learn more, find resources and connections at Maker Ed (www.makered.org), a nonprofit organization that supports educators and communities—especially those in underserved areas—in their efforts to facilitate meaningful making and learning with youth. Sylvia Martinez and Gary Stager, coauthors of *Invent to Learn: Making, Tinkering, and Engineering the Classroom* (2013), provide an overview of the tools and strategies that are fueling the maker movement in schools globally (www.tinyurl.com/hdn8rxj). Follow #makered.

Personalized learning. Starting from the belief that not all students learn alike, personalized learning encompasses a wide range of technologies, assessment and reporting tools, and teaching practices to help each student succeed. To learn more, explore the working definition of personalized learning developed by iNACOL (www.tinyurl.com/h3t8rpu), which describes four pillars: learner profiles describing each student's strengths and needs, competency-based progression toward mastery, personal learning paths; and flexible learning environments. Follow #personalizedlearning.

Project-based learning (PBL). Students gain academic knowledge and develop critical thinking, collaboration, and other skills by investigating or responding to an open-ended question, problem, or challenge (often with real-world connections). They typically apply their understanding to create something new, teach others, or advocate for a solution. To learn more, explore the elements of high-quality PBL defined by the Buck Institute for Education (www.bie.org/about/what_pbl). Follow #pblchat.

THE URGENCY OF CHANGE

The need for school change has been well established. As early as 1997, a year before the launch of Google, Roland Barth, founding director of the Principals' Center at Harvard University, urged educators to heed the new demands of the Information Age. Students in the mid-20th century graduated from high school knowing 75 percent of what they would need to know to be successful in the workplace. That number would plummet to 2 percent in the 21st century, he predicted, because of the explosion of information (and the advent of "Googling," which he had not anticipated). Well-prepared students would be those who possess "the qualities and the capacities of insatiable, lifelong learners, capable of framing questions, marshaling resources, and pursuing learning with dedication, independence, skill, imagination, and courage" (Barth, 1997, p. 56).

P21, the Partnership for 21st Century Learning, has been advocating a similar profile of well-prepared learners since its founding in 2002. This nonprofit consortium has made the "4Cs"—communication, collaboration, critical thinking, and creativity—a widely recognized shorthand for describing the skills that students need to develop, in addition to academic understanding, to be ready for the challenges ahead in college, careers, and citizenship.

Figure 1.1   P21 Framework for 21st Century Learning has made the 4Cs a commonly recognized shorthand for these essential skills: critical thinking, communication, collaboration, and creativity.

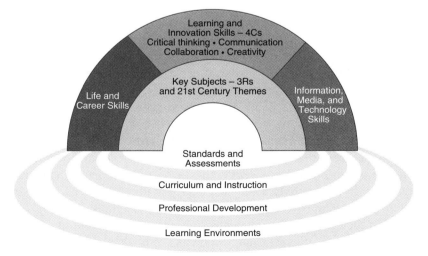

Source: P21, Partnership for 21st Century Learning.

We continue to hear variations on the same themes, both from within and beyond education. Yong Zhao, global education expert from the University of Kansas, adds to the preceding list of competencies an entrepreneurial mindset. He describes our traditional education model as "employee oriented" (Zhao, 2014, p. 185). It focuses on transmitting a body of knowledge and skills that have been predetermined to be valuable. Not surprisingly, this model values uniformity, consistency, standardization, and an emphasis on outcomes. Entrepreneur-oriented education, in contrast, aims to help students discover and build on individual passions. Instead of preparing them to be reliable employees for predictable jobs, an entrepreneurial education prepares students to be job creators and social innovators (Zhao, 2014).

Jaime Casap, global education evangelist for Google, offers more insights about how the world of work has shifted due to specialization and the need for collaboration:

> If I told [Google CEO] Larry Page that I had finished a project without consulting anyone else, I probably wouldn't keep my job much longer. Google is a project-based organization. We live in a project-based world. Collaboration is how we get things done. (Casap, 2015)

IBM's survey of CEOs from around the world echoes these familiar wishes for what employers want in employees: collaborative, communicative, creative, flexible thinkers (IBM, 2012).

Students themselves offer more perspective about what's missing from K–12 education. Data on student engagement paint a worrisome picture (Kuh, 2007). Only 50 percent of students feel engaged in school, according to the Gallup Student Survey of students in Grades 5 through 12. That leaves every other seat in our classrooms filled by a student who is either not engaged (29%) or actively disengaged (21%; Gallup, 2015). What's more, fewer than half of today's students report feeling hopeful about their own future; 34 percent feel "stuck"; the remaining 18 percent describe themselves as discouraged about their future prospects. Curiosity—a key attribute of the innovator's mindset—also shows a steady decline as students advance from elementary into secondary grades and focus more on getting correct answers than on asking good questions.

On the brighter side, students offer clues about the kind of education that does interest them. Students report they are engaged by projects that connect the classroom with the world outside school

(Taylor & Parsons, 2011). Some 45 percent aspire to create something that will improve the world (Gallup & Operation HOPE, 2013). After hearing countless students and teachers describe the motivation that comes from doing real-world projects, the Buck Institute for Education updated its definition of high-quality PBL to include "authenticity" as an essential ingredient (Larmer, Mergendoller, & Boss, 2015).

NOT FAST ENOUGH

Despite persistent calls for school change and an expanding research base about the effectiveness of more student-centered learning practices (American Institutes for Research, 2016), education is not shifting fast enough to prepare students for the future that's right in front of them. Nearly 60 percent of first-year undergraduates discover that, despite being eligible to attend college, they are not ready for postsecondary studies. Those caught in the so-called readiness gap must take remedial courses for which they earn no college credit, pushing up the costs and lowering the odds of college completion (National Center for Public Policy and Higher Education & SREB, 2010).

Schools that break from tradition remain relatively rare, despite more than two decades of advocacy for 21st century learning. To show what school transformation looks like nationwide, P21 invites schools and districts to apply for exemplar school status. Applicants are screened by experts who look for evidence of 21st century teaching and learning. This is not a search for cookie-cutter models. Instead, P21 celebrates the unique approaches that local communities are taking to create opportunities for learning (Brown, n.d.). By 2016, four years into this initiative, only 59 of the nation's nearly 100,000 public schools had made the cut as exemplars of transformed education.

School leadership expert Eric Sheninger has coined the term *uncommon learning* to describe the pedagogies that develop "skill sets that society demands, respond to student interests, empower students to be owners of their learning, and focus on ways to create an environment that is more reflective of the current digital world" (Sheninger, 2016). Initiatives such as blended learning and PBL are among the strategies known to increase engagement, but Sheninger finds them more likely to be isolated practices than systematically embedded as part of school or district culture.

Notable exceptions are the 500 schools that are part of the Deeper Learning Network. These schools are affiliated with 10 networks that differ in some particulars but share a consistent emphasis on student-directed learning. They are places where students routinely engage in problem-solving, collaboration, and critical thinking and develop the skills of effective communicators. They integrate technology in authentic, even transformative ways rather than as substitution for paper-and-pencil tasks. They develop academic mindsets that support their journey as learners.

Some schools, such as High Tech High in San Diego, California, began as start-ups, applying project-based learning with digital tools from Day 1. Others, such as Katherine Smith Elementary School in San Jose, California, were traditional schools that have made a wholesale transformation to the New Tech Network model. By building and supporting the Deeper Learning Network and hosting an annual Deeper Learning Conference to share best practices, the Hewlett Foundation, Alliance for Excellent Education, and other allies hope to build a critical mass of schools that will effect lasting change in education. Yet, to date, the network represents fewer than 1 percent of US public schools.

Change is also afoot among the nation's independent schools, some of which are challenging long-held traditions to remain relevant for 21st century learners. The National Association of Independent Schools (NAIS) launched its Schools of the Future initiative earlier this decade to help institutions manage the tension between tradition and innovation (Witt & Orvis, 2010). Citing shifts in everything from access to information to career trends, and acknowledging the different learning styles and motivations of digital natives, NAIS also profiles schools on the leading edge of change. Unifying themes among these institutions echo patterns found in many innovative public schools, including academic rigor, project-based learning, real-world learning that extends beyond the classroom, and the integration of digital technologies. Schools that succeed in introducing these approaches typically enjoy transformational leadership and a strong culture of collaboration among both educators and students (Witt & Orvis, 2010).

No one can predict how long it will take for most schools to make the shift to some version of 21st century learning. Technology integration is certain to be part of the future-of-learning story, but we know that tech alone won't be enough to transform teaching and learning. The Organization of Economic Cooperation and

Development (OECD) reports that investments in educational technology have failed to produce hoped-for gains in student learning or to bridge the achievement gap (OECD, 2015).

Pockets of school innovation remain more typical than wholesale reinvention, and for understandable reasons. Schools that perform well, according to standardized assessments and college admissions, are often reluctant to change. Instead of feeling pressure to innovate, they remain tied to traditions that have worked well in the past. Chronically underachieving schools, meanwhile, are more likely to feel pressure to catch up rather than to innovate, even though the goals they are chasing may already be outdated or insufficient to serve today's learners.

FAIR QUESTIONS

When schools do start to prototype and tinker with tradition, they can face questions from all sides. Parents, potential allies from the business community, and other stakeholders may raise concerns or express skepticism. Teachers, too, can be resistant to change if they don't feel prepared to adopt unfamiliar pedagogies or integrate new technologies. Students who have succeeded at the old textbooks-and-tests model of learning may question why familiar routines are being upended.

When schools redesign traditional practices, policies, and facilities to better meet the needs of today's learners, they no longer look and feel the way that most of us remember. Questions naturally arise: *Why are classrooms so noisy and active? Why are students working in teams? Why don't report cards look the way I remember? Why are kids out in the community instead of sitting in class? Is all this technology use a good thing? And what about project-based learning—is it rigorous enough?*

A school superintendent recently told me about her experience of leading her community through a planning process to create a facility intentionally designed for 21st century learning. Participants on a design team began with a book study of *The Third Teacher* (OWP/P Architects et al., 2010), which describes the relationship between school architecture and learning. On a learning journey, they visited other reimagined schools as well as workplaces in their community. They asked hard questions and participated in a series of brainstorming charettes facilitated by architects.

The final product looks nothing like the familiar egg crate school layout that most of us know well, with long hallways leading to individual classrooms. Instead, classroom walls open like garage doors into a central learning commons. Furniture comes in a variety of shapes and can be rearranged in moments. Writeable walls capture students' thinking. Teachers share a collaboration space that fosters cross-disciplinary teaming. Everything about the multi-age building invites more active, collaborative, student-centered learning.

The superintendent told me she can tell within moments how visitors respond to this dynamic environment and the collaborative, active style of teaching and learning that it fosters. Parents and other visitors who had a hand in the design "get it" and lean in to see student-centered learning in action. Visitors who are unfamiliar with why and how education is changing often look perplexed. Some even stop short at the entrance, wondering if they're in the right place. This doesn't look like any school they ever attended.

Although questions remain about the best way to launch, lead, and sustain change, one conclusion is clear: School systems can't hope to make significant shifts in teaching and learning in isolation from their communities. The broader public, students included, must be engaged in conversations about how and why education is evolving. More than ever, schools need partners—inside and outside the building—who share and shape their vision. Buy-in from the entire community is essential if students are going to have opportunities to take part in meaningful, real-world learning that extends beyond the classroom. Having stakeholders on board not only accelerates change but may be the only way to sustain new ideas for the long game.

CATALYSTS FOR CHANGE

Although the call for 21st century learning dates back more than two decades, new catalysts for change are accelerating the adoption of more innovative approaches to teaching and learning and setting the stage for increased stakeholder engagement. Let's examine the catalysts that are driving school change in communities around the globe, including many of the examples you will encounter in the following chapters. Some catalysts have to do with policy; others relate to facilities and technology access. In other instances, a local issue such as a change in employment patterns or a brain drain of talented youth becomes a spark for reimagining school. As you consider these trends, think about which are most likely to concern or engage your stakeholders.

Rigor, readiness, equity. Perhaps the most consistently heard challenge for education today is the call *for all students* to be ready for college, careers, and citizenship. Achieving this ambitious goal means closing the persistent achievement gap and increasing high school graduation rates. It means expanding the college pipeline with students who may be the first in their families to pursue postsecondary education. It requires providing essential supports and alternative pathways for students at risk of disengaging from school. In communities that are taking up this challenge, the drive for rigor, readiness, and equity is proving to be a catalyst for school change. Examples in the coming chapters will illustrate why creating a climate of achievement can be a driver of wholesale school transformation (Brown, n.d.).

At both the federal and local level, expectations are changing when it comes to what students should know and be able to do. The federal Every Student Succeeds Act, reauthorizing the Elementary and Secondary Education Act (ESSA), is a catalyst for teaching and assessing more than content. ESSA calls for assessments of learning that emphasize higher-order thinking skills and understanding. It also specifically calls for family engagement to help students succeed in school.

The Common Core State Standards emphasize critical thinking, creative problem solving, and collaboration along with academic mastery. To become proficient at these skills, students need experiences that go beyond rote learning. At the same time, yesterday's bubble tests are being replaced by more comprehensive assessments—portfolios, projects, and extended performance tasks—that ask students to apply their understanding.

Technology integration. Fewer than 30 percent of US schools currently have the bandwidth they need to teach using today's technology. Federal and state efforts are expanding this capacity to ensure that at least 99 percent of the nation's students have access to high-speed Internet in their schools within the next five years, according to the Future Ready School initiative supported by the US

Department of Education and the Alliance for Excellent Education. Such connectivity has the potential to transform the educational experiences of all students, regardless of their background, but only if districts are strategic about instruction and professional development needed to take full advantage of technology.

Facility makeovers. School facilities are ripe for redesign in many communities. The Report Card for America's Schools ranks the condition of our public schools at a D+. The average age of public school facilities is approaching the half-century mark (Alexander & Lewis, 2014). There's an urgency to update or replace facilities designed for baby boomers with learning spaces that will remain relevant for the next 50 years. Initiatives underway to address infrastructure issues are a catalyst for redesigning pedagogy along with facilities.

We'll hear more in later chapters about Design for Learning, a national initiative to reimagine school, including everything from the style of instruction and integration of technologies to the design of learning spaces and furniture. Ron Bogle directs this effort for the American Architectural Foundation. His organization deliberately looks for district partners that are willing to lean into change, whether they are starting from scratch or remodeling an existing facility. "If a district leader or school board is happy with the way things are, then we can't have much impact," Bogle told me. "We look for systems where, from top leadership to the classroom, people are hardwired to do something innovative. The desire for change is shared by teachers, principals, parents, and other partners. They're all part of it." The goal of Design for Learning is to work with the willing to create "many examples of what school change looks like." Those reimagined schools will then become laboratories that others can learn from, catalyzing more change.

Not every school redesign effort requires a bulldozer. Increasingly, schools are tinkering with existing buildings by adding makerspaces, labs for hands-on STEAM (science, technology, engineering, arts, and math) learning, and media centers for creating digital content to augment library stacks. Each of these redesign efforts, when combined with a shift in instruction, offers another catalyst for change. The instructional shift, however, is more critical than the new spaces.

Design thinking. Design thinking, an open-ended process for problem solving, offers the potential to engage students as innovators in the classroom. Educators who become fluent in design thinking are also using this process to find innovative solutions to a wide range of challenges, from rethinking academic calendars to reducing high school dropout rates. Several of the examples in the chapters ahead incorporate design thinking as a strategy to better understand issues from the user's perspective. The focus on empathy, user-centered design, and rapid prototyping to overcome challenges makes design thinking another catalyst for school change.

External pressures. Pressures and questions from the larger community also can be catalysts for rethinking education. For example: How does a school remain relevant if a community's major employer closes its doors, changing job prospects for future graduates? How can school leaders respond to turbulent economic conditions, such as the recession and housing crisis at the end of the last decade? How can schools be agile enough to respond to demographic changes? How might a community prevent a brain drain or outmigration of talented youth? In future chapters, we'll hear about communities that have turned external pressures and even potential crises into opportunities for school change.

Worth Asking

Examples in coming chapters will illustrate how school systems are catalyzing change with the engagement of stakeholders. As you begin reading, consider these fundamental questions that are driving change in a wide range of settings:

- When a world of information is at our fingertips, what's worth knowing?
- Why are the basics no longer enough?
- How do we prepare students for success in a world marked by change and complexity?
- Why the increasing emphasis on teamwork and collaboration?
- Which approaches among the practices discussed in this chapter seem like the best fit for your community?

Takeaways and What's Next

Although the need for education change has been well established, school transformation has been a slow process. Several catalysts are now accelerating the pace of change. As schools consider potentially disruptive instructional practices, stakeholders need to understand the purpose and value of shifting away from traditional teaching and learning. Building common understanding of student-centered practices ensures more productive discussions and sets the stage for buy-in among diverse stakeholders. In the next chapter, we will look at stakeholder engagement strategies that have sparked widespread community support for school innovation.

CHAPTER 2

How will we engage the willing?

> "We live in a world in which we need to share responsibility. It's easy to say, 'It's not my child, not my community, not my world, not my problem.' Then there are those who see the need and respond. I consider those people my heroes."
> —Fred Rogers (from *Mister Rogers' Neighborhood*)

When Gregg Behr arrived in Pittsburgh, Pennsylvania, in 2006 to become the executive director of the Grable Foundation, he didn't realize that he was about to catalyze a grassroots effort to reinvent learning. The philanthropy focuses its grant-making efforts on improving the lives of children across the region. To get acquainted with his new community, Behr met with a variety of youth-serving organizations. As he sat down with teachers, school leaders, museum directors, librarians, and others who work with children and young people in both formal and informal education, he asked about their key concerns and challenges. He recalls feeling "dumbstruck" to hear nearly everyone he met say something similar: "I'm not connecting with kids the way I used to" (Boss, 2016a, p. 16).

That refrain sparked his curiosity, which in turn has sparked an extended—and highly productive—community conversation about rethinking education to better meet the needs of today's digitally connected learners. Within a decade, the Pittsburgh region has emerged as a national model for innovation in education. In schools and community settings, youth are now learning by making and coding, creating and connecting. Teachers are learning, too, through hands-on professional development in everything from robotics to game mechanics to kinesthetic learning facilitated by motion-capture technology. In 2014, Pittsburgh became the first US city to win the Tribeca Disruptive Innovation Award. Three districts in the region are showcase sites for the Digital Promise League of Innovative Schools. The MacArthur Foundation awarded Pittsburgh $500,000 to join Chicago and New York City in creating a "hive learning network" to support nontraditional youth programming. Connecting all these initiatives is a cross-sector network called Remake Learning. It has grown organically to include some 250 organizations and more than 2,000 individual stakeholders, united by their commitment to make leaning more relevant and engaging.

In this chapter, let's take a closer look at stakeholder engagement strategies that have generated compelling results in diverse communities, including Pittsburgh; Cedar Rapids, Iowa; and Dallas, Texas. We will see that in some communities, like Pittsburgh, a catalyst from outside traditional education sparks conversation about school change. In others, veteran educators have guided their communities to boldly reimagine school. As you read these stories, ask yourself: What would it take to catalyze conversations about school change in my community? And just as important: What's preventing us from engaging in catalyzing conversations?

REMAKE LEARNING: UPDATING THE NEIGHBORHOOD

Remake Learning emerged organically from community conversations about the future of education. Gregg Behr sparked the first such discussions by reaching out to some of the nation's leading experts in the field of learning sciences to ask, "What are we learning about learning?" That turned out to be just the right question at just the right time. He began hearing about young people pursuing knowledge outside of traditional school, leveraging technology, peer learning, and community resources in new ways. Groundbreaking research by Mizuko Ito and others in the connected learning field, for example, helped him think differently about how, when, and with whom young people learn (Ito et al., 2009). He remembers one such meeting at Carnegie Mellon University in Pittsburgh, right in his own backyard, where he met with gamers and technologists eager to help kids learn in new ways.

To build on these discussions, the Grable Foundation began hosting informal breakfast meetings open to anyone who wanted to talk about the future of learning. The invitation drew people of diverse backgrounds—teachers, parents, librarians, gamers, museum staff, roboticists, cognitive scientists, superintendents. "The conversations were so resonant," Behr recalls, "that everyone who came to one meeting thought of three or four people to invite to the next one."

A welcoming, sometimes even playful tone helped to open these big-tent conversations to people of diverse backgrounds. At one event, held in the basement theater of the Pittsburgh Children's Museum, individuals had exactly three minutes on stage to describe their vision for the future of learning. When time was up, the moderator struck a gong on loan from the symphony, symbolizing a call to action (Behr, n.d.).

Eventually, the cross-sector conversations sparked ideas for projects that had potential to change the game for young people across the region. To test nascent ideas, the Grable Foundation offered to fund small seed grants. In what turned out to be a strategic move, the philanthropy entrusted grant management to a local nonprofit called the Sprout Fund. (In later chapters, we'll hear more about some of the initiatives that have emerged—such as portable makerspaces, media labs, motion-capture technology for kinesthetic learning, and hands-on professional development to help teachers get comfortable with change.)

The Sprout Fund brought expertise in managing what director Cathy Lewis Long describes as catalytic projects. That means the organization understands how to recognize and support early-stage innovation. At the same time, the Sprout Fund does not advocate a particular philosophy or agenda for education. "We can be honest brokers," Long explains, "and amplify the voice of the network without inserting our own point of view into the work."

The Sprout Fund's role has expanded over the intervening years to include resource development, field building, and storytelling to sustain and grow the Remake Learning network. A good example of its field-building work is the *Remake Learning Playbook* (www .remakelearning.org/playbook/), a publication that documents best practices and case studies from across the network. The Sprout Fund describes this digital publication as its effort to "open source the project code for learning innovation ecosystems."

Meanwhile, the Allegheny Intermediate Unit (AIU), a regional services provider serving 42 public school districts in western Pennsylvania, has emerged as another key player in the network. AIU provides the hands-on professional development that teachers need to get comfortable with new instructional approaches or unfamiliar technologies, such as interdisciplinary STEAM projects or robotics.

The cross-sector collaboration that has enabled Remake Learning to grow and thrive offers lessons for other communities. Importantly, no one organization owns the network or sets its agenda. The Grable Foundation was a catalyst, to be sure, but was quickly joined by other organizations, individuals of diverse backgrounds, and, eventually, more funders. "There's no reason every community in the country couldn't do what we've done," says Behr. "You may not have 200 potential partners, but you probably have schools, libraries, businesses, and a community college." And "that's enough," he says, for local leaders to "think collectively about helping kids be future ready."

Indeed, collaboration has become part of the DNA of the region. "We've learned that we're better off when we do the work together," Behr says. In previous decades, when the Rust Belt region was closing steel mills and shedding factory jobs, collaboration helped stakeholders reinvent the economy around health care, higher education, and technology. Now, the same spirit has brought together people of diverse backgrounds to reinvent learning.

Worth Asking

Here are questions to consider as you think about the Remake Learning example:

- In Pittsburgh, Greg Behr's curiosity sparked initial conversations, which then expanded as more people and organizations became involved. Breakfast meetings set an informal, non-academic tone for early discussions, enabling people from disparate backgrounds (gamers, roboticists, librarians, educators) to find common ground. A sense of shared inquiry built momentum, keeping the conversations going and growing. What (or who) might be the catalyst for similar conversations about learning in your community?

- The Sprout Fund has played an important role as network builder. Is there a person or organization that could serve in the role of "honest broker" for a network in your community?
- Which organizations and individuals in your community might be interested in joining a similar conversation? How could you expand the circle to include those who aren't directly involved in K–12 education but who care about the future of learning?

IOWA BIG: RECOGNIZING THE DISCONNECT

Throughout more than two decades as a teacher, school district administrator, and entrepreneur in Iowa, Trace Pickering has been interested in questions that have the potential to shake up traditional notions of school. For example, what if school systems considered what students know and can do rather than counting how many minutes they spend in class? "For the bulk of my career, I've been interested in ideas like outcome-based education, competency-based education," he says. "It just never seemed to be the right time to make anything happen."

The opportunity for change presented itself in 2012, when Pickering had an interesting discussion with the head of a media company. Chuck Peters, president and CEO of *The Gazette* in Cedar Rapids, Iowa, had been pondering the future of newspapers in the digital age. Yesterday's subscribers now have information available 24/7, via devices that fit in their pockets. How will local news organizations remain relevant in this new era? "He told me that he thought the media problem and the school problem are the same. Both institutions are so steeped in traditions and assumptions about how things are supposed to work that it's hard to imagine anything different," Pickering remembers. Meanwhile, the world around them is changing rapidly.

That conversation turned out to be a seminal moment in the development of a radically reinvented high school called Iowa BIG. But before Pickering and others could even start to imagine a new school model, they needed to find out what others in the community were thinking about the future of learning. Stepping outside traditional K–12 structures, Pickering joined *The Gazette* in the role of community builder. His first assignment: Change the conversation about education in our community. The problem, as he saw it, wasn't a lack of fresh ideas but rather a lack of community will to support innovation. "In the past, when educators tried to make a change or do something different," Pickering says, "they suffered internal pressure [within school systems] from people who didn't want to change. Then our community would reject the idea because they didn't recognize the value of it."

He found an ally in Shawn Cornally, an innovative teacher and blogger, who had been experimenting in his own Iowa classroom with nontraditional ideas for student-centered learning. Together, they brainstormed ideas "to get the community engaged to tell us what they want," Pickering says. "Our theory was, if we design what people say they want, then they should be willing to stand up and defend it."

At first, they tried simply talking with community members about the need for school change. Informal discussions would begin with an invitation for people to describe the skills that students need to be ready for the future. From one group to the next, answers were consistent with big-picture thinking about 21st century learning: know how to collaborate; learn that failure is a good thing; be able to communicate and work with diverse people; find information quickly; build a network.

Then they would ask, So what do schools need to do to achieve those results? Once again, the answers were consistent. From group to group, people suggested ideas such as longer school days, tougher standards, more Advanced Placement classes, better teachers. "Shawn and I would look at each other and think, those are all non-solutions!" Pickering says. "Nothing you're advocating has any chance of producing the results that you say you want." How could they help community members recognize the disconnect in their thinking?

To think more strategically about community building, Pickering drew on the insights of Peter Block, coauthor of *The Abundant Community* (McKnight & Block, 2010) and other books about organizational change. Instead of a top-down approach, Block encourages stakeholders to work together to cocreate the future they desire. Cornally, meanwhile, found inspiration in an old Adam Sandler movie. What if, like the lead character in *Billy Madison,* adults in the community were sent back to school? What if they weren't treated as adult visitors, but literally walked in students' shoes? How might that shift their thinking? "Let's give them books, pencils, and a schedule to follow. Then let's have a conversation," Pickering agreed.

Over the next several months, about 50 diverse citizens agreed to be part of what became known as the Back-to-School Project. "We had people one year out of college and one year from retirement, business magnates and nonprofit leaders, a Democratic legislator and head of the county Republican Party. Men, women, all ethnicities," Pickering says. The experience was carefully planned, facilitated, and documented. In cohorts of six to eight, participants were randomly assigned to spend a half day in one of the seven area high schools that agreed to take part in the experiment. After each cohort completed its student shadowing, participants met with Pickering and Cornally to debrief their experience.

Discussions followed a pattern. The first debrief question: As an adult, what do you need to know and be able to do in life to be successful? That question generated the previously mentioned list of skills and dispositions needed for 21st century success. Next, participants discussed: How much of that list did you experience during your half day as a "student"? Most adults found little overlap between their wish list and the reality of high school.

Across all cohorts, stakeholders consistently voiced three observations from their back-to-school experiences:

- Too many students seem bored or disengaged in school.
- Teaching quality varies, but most teachers seem to be working hard to make content interesting and engaging.
- Learning in content silos—and being shuffled from one subject to another—makes no sense, based on how adults experience the world. Pickering heard many participants ask, "Why are kids so bored and teachers working so hard to engage them? We think it's because school has stripped away the context."

Finally, participants were invited to start fresh and imagine a version of school that would lead to the profile that they want to see in graduates. Across cohorts, a new vision emerged: design a school focused on student passions. Give students real work to do. Get them out of classrooms and into the community. "They told us, we aren't sure how, but we want schools to produce passionate people who love what they're doing," Pickering says. "Adults understand that when you're passionate, you're willing to do the hard work, suffer through failure, and persist when challenged." Community members also saw the value that students could add, if their energies were focused on local problem solving. "They told us, our communities have more problems than we'll ever get to solving. Why aren't we engaging our 5,000 high school students in these real challenges?" What's more, stakeholders predicted that stronger ties between youth and community could help to counter the region's brain drain.

Those conversations shaped the Iowa BIG model, which is based on passion, projects, and community. The high school program launched in 2013 as a pilot, with a dozen students and a smattering of community partners participating. By the 2015–2016 school year, enrollment was at 100, with as many as 200 students expected to apply for spots the following year. The Iowa BIG experiment has found a permanent home within the Cedar Rapids Community School District, where Pickering is now associate superintendent.

Students from seven high schools across the region (including Cedar Rapids) now spend part of their school day working with community partners on real-world, interdisciplinary projects. They meet

Figure 2.1   In the Iowa BIG model, learning is not measured by seat time. This infographic helps community members understand how students flex their time, based on the demands of projects they are working on.

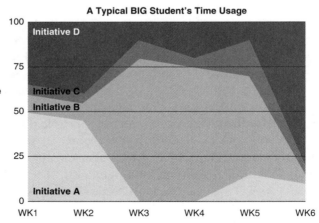

TIME *When designing Iowa BIG, our community identified **time management** as the most important skill a student can learn.*

A Typical BIG Student's Time Usage

Students at Iowa BIG **flex** their time during the week, choosing how to spend this valuable resource. Teachers and mentors provide feedback about the effectiveness of students' time-related choices. **Passion** for their initiatives is the primary driver for choosing to spend time working and learning.

Source: Iowa BIG (http://www.iowabig.org/BIG_WP/wp-content/uploads/2014/06/BIG-Visit-Day-Infographic-1.png).

in a business incubator and coworking space where they routinely interact with enterprising adults going about their work. Students choose which projects they want to join, based on their interest in compelling, real-world questions. For example: *How can we use trees to filter waste water? How can we design card games to build resilience in young people? How can we use drones to help farmers? How can we use crowdsourcing to help mycologists discover and identify unknown varieties of mushrooms? How can we help young women pursue their vision of success?* Teachers then backwards design the curriculum, mapping the skills and knowledge students will learn through each project to rigorous content standards. "It's truly students first, curriculum second," Pickering says.

WORTH ASKING

We'll hear more about the Iowa BIG model and its community partnership strategies in Chapter 7. For now, consider these questions about building community consensus:

- Iowa BIG began with deliberate efforts to change the conversation about education. Inviting stakeholders to shadow students and then debrief their experience led to more productive dialogue. What might motivate stakeholders and schools in your community take part in a similar experience? What would you hope to learn?
- In Iowa, the local media company (*The Gazette*) played a key role as catalyst, providing space for Pickering and Cornally to do community outreach and then the time and freedom to design and pilot a new model. In your community, who are the potential partners from outside education who might play a similar role? What might you gain by moving this conversation outside traditional school structures?
- The Iowa BIG team was transparent about its community-building efforts, documenting the data that emerged from the Back-to-School Project on a website (www.iowatransformed .com). These artifacts help to tell the "origin story" of Iowa BIG, underscoring the common community vision behind the school. If you intend to engage your community in a similar process, how will you capture and communicate results? How will you make learning transparent?

Dallas, Texas: Putting a Face on Personalized Learning

Design for Learning brings together architects and educators to redesign schools through a highly collaborative design process. The goal is to simultaneously rethink both pedagogies and physical environments so that students experience a more personalized education suited to 21st century learning needs. While some of the redesigned schools will be brand-new facilities, many more will be older buildings retooled for new uses.

School systems that apply to participate in this initiative must be ready for disruption and collaboration. "District leadership has to be unequivocally committed to being open to doing things differently," says Ron Bogle, president of the American Architectural Foundation, which is partnering on the national school redesign initiative with funding from the Gates Foundation. "Rather than fighting headwinds of opposition, we start with the willing."

The Dallas Independent School District in Texas, serving 160,000 diverse learners, is among the first cohort of six districts to take part in Design for Learning. Within Dallas ISD, five schools had completed initial design work and moved into the implementation stage during the 2015–2016 school year. Although the resulting school models vary widely and range from elementary to secondary, they share a backstory that starts with community engagement. Let's take a closer look at one example.

A year before the doors opened on the Innovation, Design, Entrepreneurship Academy (better known as IDEA), longtime educators Sarah Ritsema and Courtney Egelston stepped away from other responsibilities in the district to lead the design team. Ritsema, during her 13 years in the district, had taught Grades 5 and 7 before becoming a high school administrator. Egelston taught English and interdisciplinary humanities to ninth and tenth graders during her six years with Dallas ISD. When the opportunity came along to propose a new school as part of the Design for Learning initiative, the two educators began with a big question: *If we could do school differently, what would we do?* Grant support gave them the luxury of a full school year to conduct research, do community outreach, and devise a blueprint to submit for district approval.

Before committing to any design specifics, Ritsema and Egelston pored over academic research, attended conferences, consulted with experts, and visited innovative schools to see different approaches in action. They settled on three broad goals:

- Provide personalized learning so that every student is appropriately challenged
- Match a community mentor to every student and arrange internships for real-world experience
- Coach students to develop the next-generation skills considered critical for careers and college

With these three pillars in place, it was time to invite community partners to fill in the rest of the picture. "We needed our partners to help us bring these priorities to life," Egelston says. Defining next-generation skills, for example, came about through extended conversations with area employers. Their insights about workplace qualifications informed the new school's rubrics for assessing skills such as collaboration.

Because of the emphasis on mentors and internships in the school design, the planners knew they had to do more than sell stakeholders on the philosophy and goals of the school. They needed to recruit partners who would commit to getting some skin in the game as mentors and collaborators.

Egelston and Ritsema drew on their own relationships with students to animate discussions about school change. "It made sense to talk about students we knew, students we had both worked with," Egelston recalls. Three stories in particular seemed to represent the struggles that many students experience in traditional high schools. Here's how Egelston describes these students:

Ricardo is cool, but he struggles academically because of language gaps. He needs more time to develop English fluency. Amanda is a high-performing student who will do anything you ask, but she has a lot of anxiety and apprehension about the future. She will be the first in her family to go to college. She wants to become a lawyer but lacks connections and role models who could help her. Then there's Nick. He's just a character. He hates school. He thinks it's boring. He would rather work on his side businesses that use his creativity.

Ricardo, Amanda, and Nick were not composites or fictional characters. These were real kids who struggled with school for

different reasons. Sharing their stories—complete with photos—
became an effective way to communicate with audiences about the
need for new school models that would better meet the needs of students (students gave permission to have their stories shared). "When
we met with community members and potential partners, these
stories painted a picture. Then we could talk in more depth about, so
what kind of school would work for all three kids [and others like
them]?" Egelston says.

Through the extended community outreach and planning process, Ritsema and Egelston honed their own skills of communication
and collaboration. Coincidentally, those are two of the next-
generation skills they want to develop in their high school students.
In hindsight, they can point to these strategies for engaging stakeholders in shaping the vision for the new school:

- **Be flexible.** The two educators met potential partners anywhere and everywhere. "We'd meet at 7 a.m. or 7 at night, at
  coffee shops or offices, whatever worked for them," Egelston
  says. "Our partners have extremely busy lives. We do, too, as
  educators, but we're so used to the 8 to 3:30 schedule."
- **Be clear.** To hone their message, the two educators sought
  advice from a business leader who has evaluated hundreds of
  elevator pitches. The founder of the Dallas Entrepreneur Center offered critical feedback on how to improve their pitch.
  "Our first version was so bad!" Egelston admits, but she and
  Ritsema improved with practice. "It felt awkward at first, but
  we would practice at school, in the car, on the way to meetings. We got it down to 45 seconds: this is what we're about;
  here are our three priorities; here's what we need from you."
  No education jargon.
- **Be bold.** "It's hard to ask for things," Egelston admits. She
  and Retsema got past their initial reluctance by focusing on
  the needs of students. Egelston recalls, "We'd say, if you can't
  commit right now to being a mentor or offering an internship,
  is there someone else in your network we should speak to?
  A lot of our partnerships came about through those personal
  introductions and networking."

The initial rounds of discussions not only generated a starter list
of mentors and internships but also convinced local business leaders
to endorse the IDEA model. Their backing helped to garner district

approval of the new high school. It opened in fall 2015 in a remodeled elementary building with a class of 115 ninth graders (chosen at random from an applicant pool of more than 400) and will grow by another class each year until it reaches capacity at 500 students.

Ashley Bryan, director of planning and special projects for Dallas ISD, says the IDEA leadership team "acted like a start-up. They had to hustle and pound the pavement to sell people on the idea of the school."

After working with several school design teams in Dallas, including IDEA, Bryan has become convinced of the value of the design thinking process. In particular, she has found the emphasis on building empathy for the end user to be critical for engaging stakeholders. She elaborates:

> Often when we think about school redesign, we are attracted to ideas elsewhere and models that get national attention. But the best place to start is with your students, your parents, your community. Start by understanding their needs, wants, and desires, and then design in response to that. That's how you'll build a coalition of the willing.

WORTH ASKING

- How could you use stories to help stakeholders understand school challenges through the eyes of its users—students themselves?
- Consider these three strategies: Be flexible. Be clear. Be bold. How comfortable are you with boldly asking for partners to step up? How clear are you when it comes to communicating the problems you're trying to solve? How might you refine your elevator pitch to make it more compelling?
- Design for Learning leverages the design thinking process to help educators and architects work effectively with each other and with other community stakeholders. How could you build your "muscle" with design thinking?

TRY THIS: CONVERSATION CATALYSTS

How might you start a conversation about school change in your community? Informal conversations that attracted people of diverse backgrounds were the catalyst for Remake Learning. We also heard about the use of storytelling in Dallas to engage community members in thinking about the needs of diverse students.

Here are more ideas for conversation catalysts to engage the willing in your community:

- **Film screenings followed by panel discussions.** One popular film choice for community screenings is *Most Likely to Succeed* (www.mltsfilm.org), released in 2015. The documentary starts with the big picture about challenges facing American education, then helps viewers understand project-based learning by zooming in for a close-up look at two students at High Tech High in San Diego, California.
- **Book study.** Engaging parents, teachers, and other interested community members in a shared reading can help to build a common language for talking about school change. You'll hear many examples in the chapters ahead about books that have helped to catalyze change (see Appendix C for a list of suggested titles for book study).
- **Shadow a student.** Walking in a student's shoes for a day can be an eye-opening experience for adults. In the next chapter, you'll hear how a deliberate use of that idea resulted in the opening of a break-the-mold school with strong community support. During the 2015–2016 school year, nearly 1,500 school leaders from all 50 states (and beyond the United States) took part in the Shadow a Student Challenge (shadowastudent.org), an initiative of School Retool, which advocates small steps to hack school change.
- **Social media conversations.** Many districts have turned to Twitter for ongoing conversations about school change. For example, #sd36learn is the hashtag to follow to hear about innovative teaching and learning underway in Surrey Schools, British Columbia.
- **Community events.** Host a TEDx event with a focus on school change or invite community members (including students) to tell their own stories about how and when they learn best. Kelley Tenkely, founder of Anastasis Academy in Colorado, recommends inviting stories about the future of education with the prompt, "What if . . ." She expands on this idea in a blog post (Tenkely, 2016): "Instead of 'yeah, but' try playing the 'what if' game. What if none of these constraints

were in our way? What if we could make decisions apart from the system we are in? What if we had a blank slate to dream up our perfect school? What if money was no object? What do we value that we aren't willing to compromise? What is impossible to do without?"

TAKEAWAYS AND WHAT'S NEXT

Across diverse communities, providing a quality education, updated for 21st century learners, is a widely held goal. Tapping into shared community concerns for youth offers a good starting point for school change initiatives. However, strategies that work to engage potential allies may look different from one community to the next, reflecting local context and concerns. A variety of conversation starters have been offered in this chapter to recruit stakeholders as allies. In the next section, we shift from talking about "the why" of school change to focusing on strategies for engaging diverse stakeholders in implementation so that desired changes will take hold. Get ready to tackle "the how."

PART II

The How

It takes concerted effort to develop a shared vision of what school should be and then take practical steps to make that vision a reality. Grassroots visioning processes invite the perspectives of diverse stakeholders, including teachers, students, parents, school leaders, and potential community partners. Once they are engaged as allies in school change efforts, these stakeholders can help to move action plans forward and sustain the vision for the long term.

CHAPTER 3

How do forward-looking school leaders take charge of change?

"To change the system, leaders must change the culture. . . . Culture will always trump any initiative."
—Kirtman and Fullan, 2016, p. 7

Late one winter afternoon, with a major storm barreling toward her community, a superintendent was getting ready to make a decision about school closures. She had sent her staff home early and was the last one left in the building. Just as she was making a final check of weather reports, she heard footsteps in the hallway and went out to take a look. She found a father and son, seemingly oblivious to the weather. They were enthralled by a display case in the hallway. "There it is!" the boy beamed, pulling on his dad's arm and pointing to his prizewinning artwork that had earned a place of honor in the district showcase.

The superintendent congratulated the fourth grader on his accomplishment and then invited the visitors to step into her office for a moment. "I'm just getting ready to cancel school tomorrow," she confided to the boy. "Do you want to be the one to tell everybody?" She gave him a quick explanation of how she uses an alert system to push out messages to the community. Wide-eyed, he followed her instructions to hit the send button and tell everyone about tomorrow's snow day. Despite the demands on her schedule, this busy school leader recognized the opportunity to make a student feel special and also teach a quick lesson about using digital tools to connect with the world.

Superintendents, principals, and other educational leaders have to be good jugglers to manage the moving pieces of an often chaotic system. They start each day with an agenda that's likely to go sideways before lunch. While managing budgets, personnel, compliance, schedules, and even snow days, when are they supposed to find time and attention to focus on something as challenging as school change? And how can they keep their focus on what matters most—their students?

In this chapter, we examine the qualities that distinguish managers from transformational school leaders. We take a close look at how a large district enlisted community input to map out a new vision for learning. A visioning expert offers more strategies to maximize stakeholder engagement. Finally, recognizing that today's school systems require both consistency and innovation, we explore a solution that balances necessary disruption with careful attention to day-to-day operations.

Manage or Lead?

"Most school leaders are classic managers, not change leaders," acknowledges Scott McLeod, educational leadership expert, author, and associate professor of educational leadership at University of Colorado–Denver. He's also the cocreator of a series of popular presentations about school change called *Did You Know? Shift Happens* (shifthappens.wikispaces.com). School leaders "don't feel like they have a lot of time and mind space in their jobs for innovation. Most leaders I meet want to do right by kids, but they don't have a sense of urgency about school change." Maintaining the status quo is hard enough without inviting controversy. "And guess what?" McLeod adds. "Upending a school system is a big controversy."

That sense of urgency is a hallmark of transformational school leaders. Leadership experts Lyle Kirtman and Michael Fullan (2016) argue that, if school leaders are serious about creating the new and reimagined schools that students need, they cannot afford to be consumed by traditional management responsibilities. Compliance and accountability "are about avoiding problems, not producing results" (p. 6). Change leaders, in contrast, are willing to challenge the status quo and know how to build partnerships to shape and sustain a shared vision.

Consider the qualities of a Future Ready leader. This research-based designation was developed by the US Department of Education's (USDOE) Office of Educational Technology in partnership with the American Institutes for Research. A leader who meets the Future Ready standard is, by definition, a change agent (USDOE, 2015, p. 3). He or she knows how to leverage digital tools for learning transformation and can garner broad-based support to generate and sustain change (p. 2).

Pam Moran, superintendent of Albemarle County Public Schools in Virginia, was one of the first 100 school leaders to be recognized as "Future Ready" by the USDOE. Because Moran is an active social media user, she regularly shares glimpses of the innovations underway in her district, such as learning spaces where students can create their own media or maker projects that result in students sharing their prototypes to solve authentic problems. During more than a decade, she has guided her district with a combination of what she describes as "insight and outsight" (Moran, 2015). Some ideas start locally, while others arrive from afar via social media. Change is intentional but also gradual enough to keep stakeholders from feeling as if they're in constant flux.

Listen to Moran (2015) articulate "the why" and "the how" of change leadership:

First, "the why":

Who doubts that young people must be ready for a future in which they will be challenged by radical workforce evolution, global problems from environmental degradation to geopolitical instabilities, and demographic shifts redefining family, community, and culture? How do we prepare learners for that? Considering how to proactively respond inside the walls of schools to the exponential changes occurring outside those walls keeps me up at night. (para. 2)

Then, "the how":

Mapping our district staff's course through these radical innovations pushes me to look outside traditional education resources as we prepare our kids for adult life. I've come to realize that as a leader, it's not just **insight**—my own observations and understandings—that informs what our district must do to catalyze learning and unleash the potential of educators and young people. Listening across a flattened hierarchy to the valuable perspectives of students, parents, educators, and community members also illuminates the paths that we must take. And I've come to understand that the best strategic decisions emerge by paying attention to how the world is changing beyond the perspectives gleaned from inside my educational community and from my own intuition. **Outsight**, *the power or act of seeing external things clearly, also matters.* (para. 3)

INCLINED TO ACT

Change leaders don't try to upend entire systems all at once. Instead of pursuing laundry lists of initiatives, they tend to focus on "skinny plans," according to Kirtman and Fullan (2016). Nor do they schedule meetings for the sake of meetings or empanel committees whose recommendations will only get shelved. Instead, they look for opportunities to act.

When Brett Jacobsen arrived as the head of school at Mount Vernon Presbyterian School in Atlanta in 2009, the region was reeling from the recession and housing crisis. Enrollment was in decline at the independent school, which had added a high school to its more established preK–8 offerings shortly before the economic downturn. Those conditions, largely caused by external factors, created the opportunity for change inside the school.

To prepare for his challenging new role, Jacobsen immersed himself in research about change leadership, both within and beyond education. One of the books that resonated with him was *The First 90 Days: Critical Success Strategies for New Leaders at All Levels* (2003) by Michael Watkins, which inspired him to think of his school as a start-up. He knew that at the relatively young high school, in particular, "there wasn't systemic inertia. In many ways, we were starting with a clean slate."

Applying what marketing experts Kim and Mauborgne call "blue ocean strategy," he looked for ways to differentiate the school rather than delivering the same model already available at other institutions in the region. "We didn't want to be known as another traditional college prep school. That's a model that's on the way out. But we didn't necessarily want to be known as a progressive school, either. We starting thinking about pulling from existing tenets along with emerging ideas to create something new. We wanted to shape our brand and shape the narrative around our brand."

Looking for a place to take action, the new head of school focused first on revising the school's mission statement. The previous mission statement seemed to have little traction beyond the school website. The new statement, adopted by the school board, begins: "We are a school of inquiry, innovation, and impact." Jacobsen selected each of those three *i* words as a call to action. Inquiry demands questioning. Innovation requires creative problem solving. Impact involves making a difference that matters.

Figuring out how to make those concepts come alive in the classroom has helped to drive the school's transformation over the past seven years. In building a new leadership team for the school, Jacobsen has deliberately sought colleagues who share a similar inclination toward action. "I looked for builders, not sustainers," he says. "I wanted idea generators."

Change has been ongoing. One milestone was the development of a conceptual map known as the Mount Vernon Mind (see Figure 3.1). Developed through a collaborative process, it defines six mindsets that the school considers to be essential for 21st century success: Solution Seeker, Ethical Decision-Maker, Communicator, Creative Thinker, Innovator, and Collaborator.

The whole staff was involved in identifying and defining these competencies, starting with a book study of *The Global Achievement Gap* (Wagner, 2010) to ensure that everyone had shared understandings and common language. Feedback sessions gave teachers opportunities to voice their ideas when the mindsets were still in draft. A team then came together to synthesize feedback and research into a concise model that would apply across the school. Early drafts were revised again, based on more staff feedback, before Jacobsen introduced a final version. That work set the stage for another round of collaborative work, focusing on how to assess the mindsets and give students feedback on their growth. This iterative process is indicative of how the school moves forward and reflects a schoolwide use of design thinking. Explains Jacobsen, "We'll ship an idea, troubleshoot, and then ship it again."

Figure 3.1 The Mount Vernon Mind, developed through a collaborative process, comprises six competencies considered essential for 21st century success.

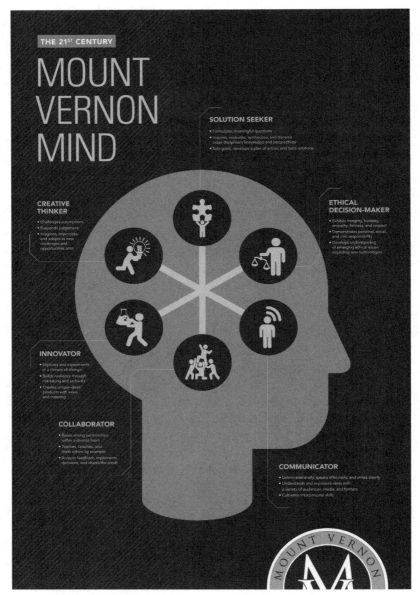

Source: Mt. Vernon Presbyterian School (http://www.mvifi.org/blog/2016/08/08/beyond-the-buzzwords-making-meaning-of-the-mindset).

The Mount Vernon Mind is a good example of what EdLeader 21 calls a profile of a graduate. A national network of school and district leaders focused on integrating the 4Cs (communication, collaboration, critical thinking, and creativity) into education, EdLeader21 encourages its members to work with stakeholders to produce a description of their ideal graduate. To date, dozens of districts across the country have taken up this challenge. Stakeholder conversations typically focus on the essential skills that all students will need for life and work in the 21st century. Capturing that description in graphic form makes it memorable and easy to communicate to diverse audiences, including students. (Resources to help schools and districts develop a profile of a graduate are available at www.profileofagraduate.org.)

Design thinking has become a schoolwide strategy that inspires action. "It's part of the DNA of the school, how we move organizationally, operationally, and in the classroom," Jacobsen says. He first encountered design thinking several years ago at a national education conference and immediately saw the connections to his school's aspirations. "I walked out of that session thinking, we can do this," he recalls. To introduce the approach back on his campus, he didn't empanel study groups or conduct extensive research: "We put it in the hands of students." Specifically, it was "Lower School," or elementary, students who began using the process to tackle interesting challenges in their community. For example, first graders redesigned a bus stop near campus to improve the public transit experience for commuters. The Lower School designated a very visible classroom as its design thinking lab, where students had access to prototyping materials and room to work collaboratively. "That space became a live lab. Other teachers would walk by and think, I can do that with my students," Jacobsen explains.

The approach has spread from there to all grade levels and all staff. High school engineering students, for example, used design thinking and a 3-D printer to build a prosthetic hand for a college freshman. The entire school community used the same process to imagine what they wanted in a new high school campus. The school now introduces others to design thinking by hosting an annual conference. "It's not window dressing," Jacobsen says, but rather fuel for strategic action.

How else do school leaders who have moved their communities toward more student-centered, digital-age learning make time and space for the hard work of change leadership? Let's hear how a large district has built a collective vision through extensive community outreach.

How to Build a Collective Vision

Chesterfield County Public Schools is one of the nation's 100 largest districts, serving about 60,000 diverse learners in both urban and suburban schools near Richmond, Virginia. In 2010 when the district's previous strategic plan was nearing its end date, Superintendent Marcus Newsome invited his community to imagine how teaching and learning should look by 2020.

He knew that some community members would resist change. After all, yesterday's schools had worked just fine for them. "There were voices saying, 'Anything beyond reading, writing, and arithmetic is a waste of my tax dollars,'" Newsome acknowledges. What's more, the recession that began at the end of the previous decade had caused the district to make deep cuts in personnel. That made technology investments a hard sell, even if digital tools would open new avenues for engaged learning. When the superintendent suggested in a conversation that it might be time to invest in educational technologies, he recalls one prominent citizen's response: "Over my dead body."

Leaders of the business community, meanwhile, seemed more open to fresh thinking. "They are the end users of our 'product'— our students," the superintendent says. "They understood the need for change." Not everyone in the business community, however, was well-versed in critical issues facing public education, such as the need to address the achievement gap and close the digital divide.

As he prepared to lead the visioning process, the superintendent was ready for hard conversations. "I was determined to be transparent every step of the way. I knew we would have to do a lot of engagement and educating," he says, to develop a plan that all stakeholders would get behind and that would guide all students toward college and career readiness.

Early in the visioning process, the district hosted a series of six community forums, each featuring a prominent speaker. One month, it was a futurist talking about the advent of self-driving cars, personal robots, and meals "printed" by 3-D printers. The next month, a peace activist, astronaut, entrepreneur, or university president would discuss the capabilities young people need to thrive and adapt in a changing world.

Donna Dalton, chief academic officer for the district, remembers the buzz of conversation generated by these well-attended gatherings, which the district promoted via social media. "The speakers helped us paint a vision of what our students will need for the future," she recalls, and created common language for talking about changes and uncertainties today's students can expect. Students themselves took part in the events, and some were motivated to take an active role in planning the future of education in their own community.

Through the forums and other community events, the district developed a massive electronic mailing list of some 60,000 stakeholders. Regular communication—via e-mail, Facebook, and other platforms—kept everyone from parents to business leaders to students to teachers informed and involved as the district rewrote its vision and mission statement. The version adopted by the school board in 2011 reads as follows:

> **Vision**—Chesterfield County Public Schools will provide an engaging and relevant education that prepares every student to adapt and thrive in a rapidly changing world.

> **Mission**—Chesterfield County Public Schools, in partnership with students, families and communities, emphasizes and supports high levels of achievement through a global education for all, with options and opportunities to meet the diverse needs and interests of individual students. (Chesterfield County Schools, 2012, p. 5)

To move from these lofty goals toward action, the district engaged smaller working groups, known as Innovation Teams, for the next round of planning. With participation from parents, teachers, students, and other community members, Innovation Teams developed strategies and time lines around three specific goals: academic achievement, 21st century learning and technology, and citizenship and core values.

The strategic plan that emerged, known as *Design for Excellence 2020,* has a clear focus on students. As Dalton explains, "The plan looks at, where do we want our students to be by 2020? Which key habits do we want our students to acquire? What's a timeline that will get us there, without overwhelming our teachers?"

The crisp focus on students and academic achievement is a departure from previous strategic plans. Earlier plans tended to emphasize "what's important to people in the central office. The people at the school level did not have the same enthusiasm," Newsome acknowledges.

By focusing squarely on student learning, the district has invited teachers to see themselves as partners in school change. Their goals for professional growth are now aligned to school improvement plans, which in turn align to the district's strategic plan. Parents, too, can see how the action steps "will be in the best interests of their children," Newsome says. And students have emerged as key players in shaping their schools of the future. "When students talk, people listen," says the superintendent. During his tenure, he met regularly with a brain trust of 25 students, who served as his focus group.

With the new strategic plan in hand, Newsome was ready to move forward—fast. "What's more important than a strategic plan," he says, "is strategic *action*. With the board's approval, I was ready to put the pedal to the metal." In upcoming chapters, we'll hear more about how the district has engaged parents, teachers, and students in the shift to anywhere–anytime learning, leveraging a variety of digital tools and online resources to help students prepare for college and careers.

Each year since 2012, the superintendent has reviewed and updated *Design for Excellence 2020* so that the plan remains relevant and timely. He uses a color-coding system to communicate progress:

Green is for the initiatives in the plan that are going well and need to move full speed ahead. Yellow indicates caution; these are initiatives that may need some tweaking. Red means it's not working; we need to stop doing this. Blue is for things we have not thought about in the previous year, but where schools now need support.

In 2016, Newsome was preparing to retire after a decade of change leadership in Chesterfield County. Was every school where he hoped it would be? Was every student reaching his or her potential? Not yet. But as he prepared to hand off the reins to his successor, Newsome knew that he was leaving a district where a bold vision for the future of learning is widely shared and thoughtfully implemented.

Thinking about his final, color-coded update of *Design for Learning 2020,* he added, "It's rewarding to see so much green."

WORTH ASKING

After hearing about the community engagement process used in Chesterfield County, consider these questions about your context:

- If your community hosted forums about the future of education, who would you want to participate? Who might be compelling speakers to ignite conversation?
- How could your community build on those events to engage stakeholders? In Chesterfield County, for example, the district built a massive e-mail list, used social media to keep stakeholders informed and engaged, and formed innovation teams to move ideas to action.
- What are your strategies for keeping your existing strategic plan up to date and communicating progress to your community? Do you have a system for tracking progress akin to the color-coding you heard about in the previous example?

Creating a collective vision is a key strategy for engaging stakeholders in school change, but that's just a starting point. As we heard in the previous example, vision statements need to be followed by strategic actions or nothing happens. Once changes are set in motion, however, new questions arise: How can you maintain the consistency and predictable routines of school during periods of disruption? How much turbulence will students, teachers, and parents tolerate? In the next example, you will hear about a strategy for embedding innovation into the school culture without dismantling the routines and smooth operations necessary for effective teaching and learning.

DOES YOUR SCHOOL NEED A DUAL-OPERATING SYSTEM?

Even in this current era of rapid change, educators have good reason to be cautious about adopting the next new thing. No one wants to gamble on our students' futures. Seasoned teachers who have seen previous initiatives come and go can't be blamed for keeping their heads down, waiting for this storm to pass. Parents rightly demand assurance that new instructional approaches aren't just novel but will be qualitatively *better* for their kids.

The American School of Bombay (ASB), a highly regarded international school in Mumbai, India, has embraced the challenges that come with innovation. Since 2011, the ASB leadership team has relied on an internal research and development (R&D) department to drive change in a strategic way. R&D staff work alongside teachers (and sometimes parents, students, and other stakeholders) to research, prototype, evaluate, and scale worthy ideas. In a relatively short time, the school has managed to overhaul its academic calendar, redesign learning spaces, introduce makerspaces, and initiate instructional strategies and technologies that make learning more personal and meaningful to students. Meanwhile, the more familiar operations of school—such as budgeting, staffing, and evaluation—continue to run smoothly because the school has not eliminated or neglected these essential front-office responsibilities in its quest to innovate.

ASB describes this model as its "dual operating system" (Luthra & Hoffman, 2015, p. 17). Rather than serving competing agendas, the two systems are interdependent and mutually focused on serving the best interests of students. One system focuses on stability, the other on innovation. Superintendent Craig Johnson and his leadership team sit right in the middle, enabling R&D to be as agile as a start-up while day-to-day operations hum along.

To share its approach with other school systems, ASB has documented eight essential conditions that enable sustained innovation to become the new status quo (Luthra & Hoffman, 2015, p. 17). ASB welcomes school leaders and study groups to use the following conditions to take an innovation audit of their own institutions.

ESSENTIAL CONDITIONS FOR EFFECTIVE R&D FOR SCHOOLS

1. **Empowered leaders:** Leaders are charged and empowered to lead R&D work throughout the school. There is institutional commitment to R&D and a framework for moving ideas from prototype into the day-to-day function of school.

2. **Engaged communities:** R&D continuously engages and partners within the school community and the global community (i.e., beyond the school walls). The school provides a network for collaboration.

3. **Intrinsic motivation:** *You can't force people to change; you can only help them want to.* This philosophy translates to

practices such as voluntary, interest-based teams that come together to explore, study, prototype, research, and scale R&D work.

4. **Future connection:** A relationship with the future guides and compels R&D work today. A future-connected school is optimistic, builds pathways, and expects obstacles.

5. **Skill capacity:** Learners, inquirers, and doers are continuously growing, developing, and using their innovation skills.

6. **Resource capacity:** Resources ensure sustainable inquiries and the capacity to act on emerging opportunities.

7. **Design thinking competence:** Design thinking is embedded as a core process for research, capacity building, and innovation.

8. **Impact validity:** Valid R&D work is democratically developed, deepens understanding, and provides new answers. It relies on multiple sources and results in changed practices and beliefs that impact learning.

WORTH ASKING

As you consider the advantages and challenges of introducing a team focused on research and development, ask yourself the following questions:

- Which of the essential conditions for R&D already exist in your school or system? How robust are they? How can you tell?
- Which conditions would need to be introduced or strengthened in your setting?
- Where might you encounter resistance to R&D efforts in your school community?

TRY THIS: CHART YOUR COURSE WITH COMMUNITY VISIONING

"What are our aspirations of school?"

A big, open-ended question like this one is where a collaborative school visioning process needs to start. That's the expert advice of

Frank Locker, an architect and award-winning educational planner. Over many years of working with communities in both the United States and internationally, Locker has fine-tuned a process to help stakeholders adopt a new vision for teaching and learning to drive school change. He shared some key strategies in an interview.

Lead with questions. "What's important for kids to be learning? How should teachers be doing their work? What are the key words that describe the future of education?" When community members discuss these important questions, they often find themselves challenging traditionally held notions of school. Starting with big-picture conversations sets the stage for a more productive visioning process. Locker has heard the same big questions resonate across diverse contexts—from Rust Belt communities where yesterday's jobs have evaporated to urban centers where technologists are busy inventing the future to the Harvard University School of Education/ School of Design where he coteaches a course on innovative learning environments.

Challenge tradition. Convincing stakeholders to reconsider their fundamental view of teaching and learning may require "a major intervention," Locker acknowledges. That's especially true in communities where schools perform well according to traditional measures, including standardized tests. "Everyone expects their kids' school to reflect the schools they attended. That model still works— but only for some students," he acknowledges.

When teachers, parents, and other stakeholders confront evidence about what's needed to prepare all students for the future, they can't help but take a hard look at yesterday's model of school. A superintendent or school leader can educate constituents by circulating recommended readings, hosting a film screening, inviting guest speakers, or holding community forums to introduce key research (see Appendix C for suggested titles for book study or shared reading).

It doesn't take long for most stakeholders to recognize that the 4Cs are must-haves for future careers and more. Knowing how to communicate effectively, think critically, solve problems creativity, and collaborate with others are essential skills "that are good for civic life, for family life, for our well-being," Locker says. Yet these skills are not encouraged in school systems that emphasize rote learning and recall of content. "If you don't get people away from standardized testing as the only measure that we have of suc-cessful schools, you will never make any progress," he cautions. On the other hand, shifting to "a more well-balanced focus on the whole child opens the discussion on what we should be doing in all of learning."

If a community is ready to roll up its sleeves and rethink educa-tion, then it's time to enlist a formal visioning team for focused, col-laborative work. The process of writing a new vision statement can happen over a few days or a few months "but involves tons of care in what you're asking people to do," Locker cautions. What follows is an overview of a process he has used to advantage across diverse contexts.

Get the right people in the room. Locker offers specific recom-mendations for who should be in the room and how they should work together.

- Thirty to 50 people is a good number for a visioning team. "Any fewer, and you won't get the demographics you need to have represented in a balanced way. You need a big enough brain trust to do good work." If the team approaches 100, it gets unwieldy.
- Invite educators, but not too many. An even split between educators and noneducators is a good mix.
- Include kids—carefully. "Invite students who are comfortable speaking with adults, elementary as well as secondary. They don't have to be the best and brightest, but they need to know they have a voice. I've seen fourth graders turn whole groups on their head."
- Include parents. "Parents who have more than one child will understand that not all kids learn the same way."
- Tap creative businesses. "Look for businesses that are inno-vative, that value problem solvers, that are looking for the same qualities in employees that you are trying to create in education."
- Recruit a cross-section of the community. "People like youth pastors or camp leaders will know kids from other points of view (outside of school). You'll want a city official or town manager, too. A newspaper editor can help get the word out."

Use the workshop model. Structure the experience as a workshop, with participants in small groups and a trained facilitator at each table to keep the process on track. Keep formal presentations to a minimum. Encourage participants to spend their time on open-ended questions, such as those already suggested. Use a flip chart to capture their comments and create artifacts for future discussions. Have teams frequently report out to the whole group to keep ideas circulating.

Make it a feel-good experience. "If participants don't walk out feeling really good about the experience, then it's going to be an uphill battle going forward," Locker says. "Everything about it—the length of the meeting, not overtalking, care in asking the questions—all of those have to do with making sure people feel good when they walk out."

Engage the broader community. Once the visioning team has done its work to define a direction for the future, the next task is to engage the broader community in moving from vision to implementation. "This is the time to share the vision—not to ask permission," he says. "When you ask how to deploy, you'll get some good ideas and you'll find out who's buying in." Recruit the same people who served on the visioning team to be spokespersons or moderators for larger community conversations. Statistics and research may be useful to share, "but we're really trying to get into the hearts and minds of our constituents." Making that emotional connection helps stakeholders remain invested in planning for the future of education.

Steer clear of pitfalls. There's not one right way to lead a visioning process, but there are pitfalls to avoid. "Don't attempt to do this work and think it's just for the school board," Locker cautions. Unless teachers, parents, students, and other stakeholders are involved and invested, there's little chance of buy-in or long-term change.

TAKEAWAYS AND WHAT'S NEXT

Transformational school leaders feel a sense of urgency about the need for school change. Although effective leaders recognize the importance of attending to daily management responsibilities, they avoid getting so consumed by the details that they can't focus on the big picture. To develop a collective vision, leaders may have to navigate challenging conversations with stakeholders. Maintaining a laser focus on what's best for students helps to build consensus and maintain the support of allies. A strategy for managing change will balance the need for innovation with the necessity of smooth day-to-day operations. In the next chapter, let's consider the supports that teachers need to get comfortable and confident with unfamiliar ways of teaching and learning.

CHAPTER 4

How will we support teachers as they become 21st century educators?

"Teachers learn new ways of teaching by seeing them, understanding them, and practicing them. Professional development that includes these elements is very, very successful because of the learning capacity of teachers."
—Joyce and Calhoun, *Realizing the Promise of 21st Century Education*, 2012, p. 7

In previous chapters, we have heard about school change initiatives unfolding in a variety of ways, from community visioning events that engage diverse stakeholders to student shadowing days that put adults into students' shoes. No change effort stands a chance of succeeding, however, without the engagement and willing participation of teachers. In this chapter, let's consider how teacher engagement can be hardwired into the redesign of schools. Examples of grassroots leadership show how classroom innovators are taking good ideas to scale. Personalized learning for teachers gives them just-in-time opportunities to be learners themselves as they explore and evaluate new tools and unfamiliar strategies for the classroom. Well-designed, collegial learning experiences avoid the all-too-common pitfalls of ineffective professional development.

TEACHERS AT THE TIPPING POINT

A host of researchers have reached the same conclusion. Linda Darling-Hammond, Stanford University education professor, describes teachers as "the fulcrum determining whether any school initiative tips toward success or failure. Every aspect of school reform depends on highly skilled teachers for its success" (Darling-Hammond, 2010, p 1). Former principal Eric Sheninger puts it this way: "Teachers are the true catalysts of change that can create schools that work for kids" (2016, p. 190). The Quaglia Institute for Student Aspirations, drawing on decades of research, reminds us of the critical role of teacher–student relationships to drive learning. Educators who build positive, caring relationships with students become "heroes to their students who look up to teachers and school leaders as people to learn from and communicate with about many things" (Quaglia Institute, 2011).

Ironically, despite their essential role in student learning, teachers often feel excluded from efforts to reimagine what happens in the classroom. The Center on Education Policy (Rentner, Kober, & Frizzell, 2016) reports that most teachers believe their voices are not often factored into the decision-making process at the district (76%), state (94%), or national (94%) levels. Results are somewhat better locally, with 53 percent of teachers agreeing that their opinions are considered most of the time at the school level, but state or district policies are seen as barriers to teaching by nearly half of those in the profession.

Yet at the same time, a growing number of teachers are leveraging professional networks and digital tools to take change into their own hands. Reporting on K–12 educational technology trends for 2016, *EdSurge* identified grassroots professional development as a key driver of teacher learning. "More and more teachers are driving their own professional development through a host of digital tools, from Twitter and Facebook to individual digital materials" (*EdSurge,* 2016).

Informally organized Edcamps, for example, now occur in all 50 states, with teachers volunteering to engage in peer-to-peer learning on topics they choose (see Crib Sheet 401: Connections for Professional Learning). More than 350 unique education chats take place on Twitter each week, with the focus ranging from project-based learning (#pblchat) to maker education (#makered) to hip-hop education (#HipHopEd).

What's more, innovative classroom teachers have inspired many of the pedagogies—including flipped learning, Genius Hour, and globally connected classrooms—that are rapidly gaining traction to better engage today's learners. Professional learning networks, connected by social media, have enabled communities of practice to grow up around each of these potentially disruptive ideas.

In this chapter, we will explore two questions about ensuring that teachers are fully and intentionally engaged in shaping schools of the future. First, how are school systems making sure that teachers have a voice in defining "the why" so that visioning efforts happen *with* them rather than being done *to* them? Second, how are schools

CRIB SHEET 401

Connections for Professional Learning

Educators who are motivated to develop new teaching strategies or find classroom applications for technology tools don't have to wait for professional development to be offered in their school or district. Increasingly, they are taking advantage of informal networks to drive their own professional growth and create communities of practice around powerful ideas. Among the tools and resources for connected learning are the following:

Edcamps. Edcamps (also known as *unconferences*) are locally organized, noncommercial events where educators engage in peer-to-peer learning. Participants typically set the agenda, lead the discussions, and share their insights and reflections via social media. Since the first event took place in Philadelphia in 2010, Edcamps have engaged more than 50,000 teachers in at least 25 countries.

#edchats. Regularly scheduled chats about a wide range of educational topics use Twitter to connect and strengthen communities of practice. An online calendar tracks upcoming chats (www.tinyurl.com/kk04r25).

PLN. Unlike more structured professional learning communities (PLCs), which are often school-based and focused on a specific agenda, a personal learning network (PLN) is an individual's go-to list of online connections for insight and feedback. Social media tools connect educators across time zones and geographies, enabling them to overcome classroom isolation, connect their students for collaborative projects, and contribute to communities of practice around emerging trends in education.

rethinking "the how" so that the professional learning necessary to implement change is more personalized, collaborative, and respectful of teachers' insights and their passion to do right by their students? After all, 68 percent of teachers enter the profession because they are motivated to make a difference for students (Rentner et al., 2016). It's wasteful—indeed, foolish—not to harness this passion to improve teaching and learning.

TEACHERS SHAPING THE VISION

In the Design for Learning national initiative discussed previously, teacher engagement is bolted into the design process. Educators work alongside architects as peers in design thinking, imagining how instructional programs *and* physical spaces can be redesigned to better meet learning goals. Teacher engagement is deliberate, according to Ron Bogle of the American Architectural Foundation (AAF), because teachers largely determine whether education initiatives will live or die. In a previous research project called Voice of the Teacher, AAF interviewed teachers in diverse school settings. Schools that exemplified innovation in both instructional approaches and learning spaces tended to have been developed in collaboration with teachers. In contrast, at schools that lacked teacher engagement on the front end, teachers tended to stick with traditional instruction even if the spaces invited doing school differently (Bogle, 2013).

How can schools ensure that teachers are engaged early and often in conversations about teaching and learning? We heard earlier about teachers taking part in Innovation Teams in Chesterfield County Schools. Teachers have also been active participants in Remake Learning in Pittsburgh. Let's consider some other examples of teacher engagement in school change.

UNCOVERING TEACHER INNOVATION IN SALISBURY TOWNSHIP

In Salisbury Township School District in Pennsylvania, Superintendent Randy Ziegenfuss and Assistant Superintendent Lynn Fuini-Hetten, both longtimers in the district, are relatively new to their current leadership roles. After several years of a 1:1 initiative that had expanded access to laptops and tablets across grade levels, these district leaders were looking for evidence of transformative learning.

"How does having access to information change what we do in the classroom?" Ziegenfuss wondered. "We wanted to reinvigorate that conversation." They launched a yearlong campaign called Innovate Salisbury to develop a district vision for transformed teaching and learning by 2020. Teachers have played a key role from the start.

Early on, district leaders sought out teachers whose classrooms are known as pockets of innovation. Word-of-mouth recommendations surfaced a list of about 15 teachers. Next, they asked these innovators two questions about their practice: What were they doing [that's different from traditional instruction]? And what were we [as a district] doing to support them?

To calibrate what they meant by classroom innovation, teachers evaluated lessons that they considered to be rich learning experiences for students. As a benchmarking tool, they used the SAMR model for technology integration developed by Dr. Ruben Puentedura. SAMR—which stands for substitution, augmentation, modification, redefinition—describes a continuum of technology integration.

Figure 4.1   The SAMR model developed by Dr. Ruben Puentedura considers whether technology is being used to substitute, augment, modify, or redefine traditional teaching and learning.

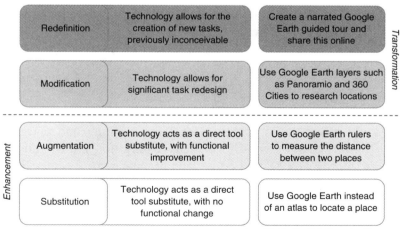

Source: Creative Commons license. Ruben Puentedura, Ph.D. (2012) www.hippasus.com/rrpweblog/.

Teachers, building leaders, and district administrators also worked together to research trends such as makerspaces and gamification. Thought leaders from outside the district were invited to take part in conversations about the future of learning, which were shared as podcasts.

The information gained through deliberate teacher engagement and action research has helped the district identify gaps and consider next steps. Teachers and school leaders have been working together to inquire into hard questions, such as these: *What keeps students from experiencing transformative learning? How could the district, individual schools, or teaching colleagues provide support to encourage more classroom innovation?* It takes patience to wrestle with these questions before jumping to answers. But by engaging teachers in the research process, Salisbury Township has increased the odds that teachers will be part of the solution.

Worth Asking

Innovative teachers often keep a low profile. I've heard more than one creative teacher extoll the benefits of working under the radar, where "nobody told me I couldn't." A challenge of change leadership is identifying early adopters and innovators and then finding opportunities to scale their good ideas. It's worth considering, then, these questions:

- How do you identify classroom innovation in your building or across your district?
- How do you recruit visionary teachers to serve as peer mentors or champions of change?

Leading From the Grassroots

In some communities, a new vision for teaching and learning starts with empowered teachers advocating for more student-driven approaches. Myla Lee, a veteran elementary teacher from Novi Community Schools in Michigan, took the initiative several years ago to transform her own classroom through a rigorous, technology-rich, project-based learning approach. Her students (and their parents) responded positively. They wanted more PBL and less test-and-textbook instruction, and not just in Lee's classroom. When parents advocated to the superintendent for similar opportunities across grade levels, he invited his pioneering teacher to support colleagues wanting to make the same transformation in their classrooms. She stepped out of the classroom and into a new role as instructional coach, working alongside teachers to help them design projects and refine their practice. Rather than calling for top-down change, the district leader set the stage for a promising approach to take hold at the grassroots (Larmer, Mergendoller, & Boss, 2015).

Similarly, at Sammamish High School in the Bellevue School District near Seattle, teachers have played a central role in shifting instruction to project-based learning with an emphasis on STEM. An Investing in Innovation (i3) federal grant provided the catalyst for a multiyear change effort, starting in 2010. The school serves a diverse population, including a large number of English learners and the district's highest percentage of special needs students. Nearly half the students quality for free and reduced lunch. In pursuing the shift in instruction, the school was sending a message about equity, neatly summarized by former principal Tom Duenwald as, "We believe in all our students" (Partnership for 21st Century Learning [P21], 2015a).

To prepare teachers to implement PBL in all classes, the school developed a corps of teacher leaders who could facilitate professional learning in-house. Experts in PBL from the University of Washington provided additional support. STEM partners in the community offered real-world connections to the curriculum. But the hard work of redesigning curriculum was left to teachers. Adrienne Curtis Dickinson, a social studies teacher at Sammamish, describes how the work unfolded (Dickinson, 2013):

> PBL course re-design occurs in a phased way across the school, as course teachers receive a year-long, one-period release to collaboratively plan new PBL curriculum. This presents a real challenge, as we are not asking our teachers to redesign a unit at a time, but to examine their entire course and redesign elements of it to increase student ownership and creatively link their content to real disciplines and contemporary problems. Design teamwork gives teachers the time and collaborative space to think about putting something new and different in their classroom. It also allows teachers to learn from each other with a focus on the student experience and deepening their own reflective practice.

When Sammamish was recognized as a 21st Century Learning Exemplar School by P21, the emphasis on teacher engagement and student collaboration were among the success strategies highlighted (P21, 2015a):

> Teacher ownership of curriculum correlates with high levels of student work and student engagement. "What curriculum looks like in the PBL classrooms is fundamentally different," says Paul Sutton, a postdoctoral researcher at the University of Washington's Institute for Science and Math Education. "The level of student engagement is off the charts. Their use of technology as a collaborative tool is outstanding."

Worth Asking

At an all-staff meeting, a group of teachers expressed an interest in project-based learning. Their principal responded by offering them readings and research so that everyone would have a common understanding and shared language about PBL. Next, he organized field trips so that interested teachers could see PBL in action in different contexts. From there, the energy and enthusiasm of this volunteer teacher cohort drove the school's shift to PBL. Think about that example as you consider these questions:

- If you are a school leader, how open are you to teachers' suggestions that might lead to school transformation? How do you help teachers move forward with ideas they want to pursue?
- If you are a teacher, where and how do you find support for ideas that you think will benefit students? What holds you back from pursuing potentially transformative teaching strategies?

Personalized Learning for Teachers

Back when they were students themselves, most of today's teachers had few, if any, chances to experience project-based learning, STEAM, maker education, or the other still-uncommon approaches that put students at the center of learning. Teacher preservice programs are evolving, but most have been slow to introduce these new pedagogies and the digital tools that go with them.

That means teachers need opportunities to be learners when schools shift to unfamiliar instructional practices. Even veteran teachers may have to ponder difficult questions: *What am I supposed to be doing in a student-driven classroom? What remains essential about the teacher's role in a makerspace or media center? When students have the world's information at their fingertips, how will they know which sources are reliable?*

Let's return to Pittsburgh and the Remake Learning Network and take a closer look at how educators are making their own meaning by investigating these challenging questions.

WHO WANTS TO LEARN?

Elizabeth Forward School District, serving 2,300 students near Pittsburgh, Pennsylvania, is one of the flagship districts recognized by the League of Innovative Schools. This small district routinely hosts visitors from around the globe who want to see what happens in a gaming academy or watch students learn math and language arts by manipulating motion-capture technology in an immersive environment known as a SMALLab (see Crib Sheet 402: SMALLab). The district has reinvented its curriculum by partnering with everyone from game designers and roboticists to university researchers. This rapid reinvention has also necessitated new learning for teachers.

The transformation of Elizabeth Forward Schools began with a crisis. In 2011, Superintendent Bart Rocco saw that the district was losing enrollment to cyber academies, charter schools, and dropouts. The larger community was facing economic challenges, as well, due to the closure of a steel mill that had been the largest employer in the region. Previous generations could count on manufacturing to provide reliable middle class jobs. That was no longer an option for Elizabeth Forward students.

In search of strategies to reengage students and prepare them for new career pathways, the superintendent reached out to experts across the region, including technology entrepreneurs and researchers. He compares his resulting awakening to a scene from Plato's *Republic.* "Schools are like those characters that are chained to the wall. We don't look beyond the walls because we can't," he says. "But once we broke the chains and went out into the world, we realized that we need to change schools because the world is changing."

There was no textbook or off-the-shelf curriculum for teaching in novel environments such as a high school gaming academy, a Dream Factory makerspace at the middle school, or a mobile fabrication lab for elementary students. The district recruited from within its own staff to find teachers willing to develop new courses and prototype teaching strategies that would leverage cutting-edge technologies, as Rocco explains:

> We interviewed teachers already working for the district and asked, who's interested? Who wants to learn? We looked for people who weren't afraid to take risks. We assured them that failure is an option, that we'll continuously learn. That's exactly what we want to model for students.

Teachers who took the lead on developing pilot programs were encouraged to collaborate, with each other as well as with technology experts. Some made site visits to see programs in action in other communities, such as YOUmedia labs in Chicago. As teachers developed new courses and teaching strategies, they shared their insights with colleagues in peer-to-peer professional development. "That has empowered a second level of leadership," Rocco says, with some former teachers moving into building-level leadership roles.

CRIB SHEET 402

SMALLab

SMALLab stands for Situated Multimedia Arts Learning Lab. In a SMALLab classroom, students play learning games by stepping into an immersive environment developed by media researchers and gaming technologists. The 3-D interface uses a ceiling-mounted projector, motion sensor cameras, floor mat, and a computer to create an environment for what researchers call *embodied learning*. Instead of sitting before a screen, students use wands and other controllers to collaborate with their peers as they manipulate physical and virtual objects through whole-body motion. For example, students might learn about angles by manipulating virtual mirrors or understand the spread of disease by trying to keep a population of virtual avatars alive during an infectious outbreak (Moore, 2014).

A New Normal

Across the Pittsburgh region, other districts within the Remake Learning Network are putting their own spin on 21st century teaching and learning. Computational thinking extends across the K–12 curriculum in the South Fayette School District, for example. Avondale Schools, meanwhile, are expanding their use of makerspaces and project-based learning. Peer-to-peer professional learning has become the new normal to help teachers keep pace with change.

A central hub for teachers to explore and exchange ideas is the Allegheny Intermediate Unit (AIU), a regional services agency that serves 42 districts. At AIU's Center for Creativity, teachers can try their hand at robotics, test-drive 3-D printers, or design wearable technologies. Teachers choose from more than 100 free classes, which might be taught by classroom colleagues, AIU staff, or even K–12 students from the region. Learning tends to be hands-on and playful, giving teachers time to explore unfamiliar tools in a low-risk setting that feels like a digital playground. Teachers who want to continue experimenting with an idea back in their own classroom can borrow digital tools from a technology lending library.

To encourage professional learning in STEAM, which is a major emphasis across the region, AIU hosts an annual STEAM showcase that's attended by hundreds of educators along with potential partners, such as technology entrepreneurs or nonprofit organizations. Schools that have received STEAM grants through AIU share projects and insights. Teachers, principals, and students talk candidly about what is working well and what's challenging, fostering a spirit of collaboration and shared learning.

Deprivatizing Teaching

When Pittsburgh Public Schools launched a STEAM pilot in 2015, Shaun Tomaszewski joined the district as STEAM education coordinator. He supports teachers in a variety of ways, such as helping to plan interdisciplinary projects, connecting teachers with community partners, and locating specialized resources. Those are all useful roles, but to really help teachers change their instructional practice, he says that "the most powerful thing is establishing safe spaces within the building for professional learning." When teachers have time and space to learn together, they can dig into questions that get to the heart of school change, such as these: *What do my students need to learn? Where are they now? How am I going to get them there?* To answer those essential questions, teachers have to be willing to open the doors on their current teaching methods—both literally and figuratively. Deprivatizing teaching can provoke feelings of vulnerability, especially in schools where teachers have had little opportunity to see their colleagues in action.

To confront those concerns directly, Tomaszewski kicked off a professional development day with a powerful TED talk by Brené Brown, a social scientist who studies vulnerability. In their debrief of the video, teachers talked about why educators hesitate to be professionally vulnerable. Fear of punitive evaluations was high on their list. Tomaszewski reassured them that his role is to support innovative teaching and learning, not to evaluate teachers. "Then we could focus on how to make our STEAM schools places where teachers can learn as professionals. If we want students to learn from failure and recovery, we need to provide the same opportunities for teachers." That conversation didn't shift school culture overnight, but it sparked more open dialogue. Not long afterward, Tomaszewski overheard teachers talking about videotaping their STEAM lessons so that they could analyze them together. That was a tipping point—when teachers showed a willingness to open their doors and share their practice.

PRINCIPALS AS LEAD LEARNERS

School leaders who are willing to learn alongside teachers model curiosity, adaptability, and the courage to learn from failure. Some leaders take part in informal learning initiatives such as edcamps, #edchats, and personal learning networks (see Crib Sheet 401: Connections for Professional Learning). Others join teachers for more formal professional learning or invite action research to improve practice. They might build a common language for problem solving by inviting faculty to tackle a design thinking challenge. When leaders invite teachers to collaborate and help lead change, they build essential grassroots support for new ideas.

Earlier, we heard from the founders of Innovation, Design, Entrepreneurship Academy (IDEA), a start-up high school focused on personalized learning and entrepreneurship in Dallas Independent School District. Because they had a full school year to plan before opening the school, school leaders could be selective about hiring. Interviews included role plays in which applicants were asked to demonstrate their ability to coach students on soft skills like collaboration. Once the school was up and running, school leaders facilitated personalized professional development with their teachers.

Courtney Egelston, assistant principal and IDEA cofounder, says those learning experiences gave her and Principal Sarah Ritsema a chance to model what they want to see in classrooms. "As teachers arrived, we did a preassessment. We used that data to put them into groups and facilitated group work tailored to their learning needs." Then the two leaders made their game plan transparent. "We would show teachers our plan and the adjustments we had made [on the fly]. We debriefed, asking, How did they feel as learners? What was helpful? What was confusing?"

Teachers at IDEA have also had opportunities to attend conferences and work with outside consultants, but Egelston sees great value in leaders stepping up to lead professional development. "It builds trust. Our teachers could see that we understand the pedagogy of personalized learning. We know how to facilitate it. We also get that it's hard." When the school leaders give feedback on lesson plans or drop by class to observe, the goal is always growth. "It's never meant to be a 'gotcha,'" says Egelston.

CHANGING THE PD FORMULA

When Chesterfield County School District in Virginia was ready to move forward on its *Design for Excellence 2020* action plans— developed in collaboration with teachers, students, parents, and other stakeholders—district leaders knew that professional learning would be key to implementation of new ideas like blended learning. "To have significant change, we had to have a deep level of professional development. We knew our teachers needed dedicated time to focus on these initiatives and develop confidence with new tools," says Donna Dalton, chief academic officer for the district.

Rather than the one-shot workshops that remain all too common in education, the district took a long view on change. "We took two years to help teachers and teacher leaders build a foundation for blended learning. Every single teacher was involved. We wanted them to have a deep understanding before we introduced the technology [with a 1:1 laptop rollout]," Dalton says.

When it was time to launch the rollout, the district hosted Camp Chromebook events. Two days of hands-on learning for teachers and school leaders took place before students received their devices.

The sessions, facilitated by technology integration specialists, were deliberately playful, evoking a summer camp vibe. Teachers learned about strategies for technology integration and had time to test-drive tools available for classroom use, such as Google apps to encourage collaboration. "That was huge for creating buy-in for teachers," Dalton says. Building on the launch, support continued throughout the school year to sustain professional learning.

Despite the benefits of long-term, collaborative, job-embedded professional development, this approach is far from the norm. A two-year study by The New Teacher Project (TNTP) found that the country's 50 largest districts spend an estimated $18,000 per teacher per year on PD but see little return on their investments. Among the shortcomings: PD that is too sporadic and too disconnected from the classroom (TNTP, 2015).

Consider what happens when teachers have the opportunity to learn about an unfamiliar pedagogy like PBL through extended professional development. The model used by the Buck Institute for Education (BIE), for example, begins with a three-day intensive workshop in which teachers use PBL methods such as peer critique and collective inquiry as they design project plans. That may get them off to a good start, but it's not enough to transform instruction. That's why BIE encourages partner districts to follow up on workshops with long-term, sustained support on site. [Full disclosure: I'm a member of the BIE National Faculty.]

To avoid common pitfalls of ineffective PD, John Larmer of BIE offers these suggestions (2016):

- Include teachers in the decision to move forward on getting PBL PD.
- Guard against "initiative fatigue" and connect PBL to other PD or school improvement efforts.
- Co-construct an answer to the "Why PBL?" question first.
- Prepare for a PBL workshop in advance (for example, with shared readings and discussions).
- Let teachers know what's expected of them.
- Provide support in the form of instructional coaching and/or professional learning communities.
- Provide support in the form of time.

Although these pointers are PBL-specific, the same advice could apply to other potentially transformative teaching and learning initiatives, such as blended learning or competency-based grading.

A different kind of immersive learning experience was experienced by a cohort of master-of-arts-in-teaching students attending an intensive summer institute at the University of Alaska Southeast–Juneau in 2016. Peter Pappas, adjunct professor (and an active edublogger—@edteck), designed the course not only to teach the content of Alaska studies but also to immerse students in project-based learning with technology. He promised his 37 students that it would not be a typical history course—no lectures, time lines, or tests. Instead, from Day 1, participants discovered that they would have to use inquiry, collaboration, and digital tools to become historians. As a final product, they would write and publish their own series of culturally responsive textbooks about the regions of Alaska.

Three weeks later, students had published six iBooks, which they offered to the public as a free educational resource. Teams of six collaborated on each book, with individual students designing a culturally responsive lesson in their content area, focused on their chosen region of the state.

How did teachers describe this professional learning experience? Here are a few responses to their final reflection prompt: *You just experienced project-based learning. What did the teacher in you learn?* (University of Alaska Southeast, 2016):

- The teacher in me learned that projects don't have to only be for the teacher/professor and that people are motivated when the product is to be used/accessed by others outside of the "circle."
- For me, the knowledge that the book was going to be published not only pushed me to work hard, it also shifted my focus slightly, from "What does the teacher want?" to "What do I want out in the world with my name on it?"
- When there is no "expert" guiding the learning process, the learning group not only has to learn the subject, but they also have to research, locate, and vet the learning materials as well. This takes more time, undoubtedly. It also creates uncertainty, even after source materials have been located because we aren't 100% sure that what we've gathered is foundational, tangential, or just plain wrong. . . . We are teaching ourselves when we collaborate, research materials, synthesize information, try to form a group voice, etc. We are learning how people learn—particularly in collaboration. And that's what we are in this program for.

Worth Asking

In an initiative facilitated by the Business Innovation Factory (BIF) in Providence, Rhode Island, teachers have taken on the role of designers to propose innovative solutions to issues facing their schools. Sam Seidel of BIF explains that the model called Teachers Design for Education (TD4Ed) works by "engaging teachers as stakeholders and empowering them as designers. Provide them with the power and tools they need be the designers of new solutions." Among the design challenges that teachers have tackled using the TD4Ed approach are imagining strategies to build students' intrinsic motivation; reframing school discipline policies to create safer, more engaging schools; and motivating teachers to comfortably use technology in their classrooms every day.

Think about these questions as you consider how you might engage and support teachers as designers in your school or district:

- Which design challenges would your teachers want to tackle? How might you identify issues needing their solutions?

- What support would teachers need? (For example, they might need training or modeling in the use of design thinking.)

- How would your school or district ensure that teachers' solutions would move forward?

Figure 4.2   Design principles from Teachers Design for Education, or TD4Ed, set expectations for collaborative design work to improve education.

TD4Ed Design Principles	
1 Provide a meaningful experience.	**4** Invigorate teachers' practice.
2 Use storytelling to highlight change.	**5** Foster sustained engagement.
3 Create value together that can't be created alone.	**6** Integrate into teachers' already busy lives.

Source: Business Innovation Factory (http://td4ed.businessinnovationfactory.com/sites/default/files/pdf/TD4Ed_DesignPrinciples_Guide.pdf)

Takeaways and What's Next

Teachers are the linchpins of school change. Indeed, many of the pedagogies cited in previous chapters have been developed by classroom innovators and improved by communities of practice. Engaging teachers in shaping a collaborative vision ensures that new initiatives will be informed by teacher insights and experiences. Leverage grassroots leadership and forums for peer-to-peer learning so that teachers have a greater voice in their own learning. When new pedagogies or technologies are introduced, avoid the common pitfalls of professional development. In the next chapter, let's shift the focus to another critical stakeholder group: students.

CHAPTER 5

How will we amplify student voice?

"Student voice is the instrument of change."
—Russell Quaglia and Mickey Corso, *Student Voice:*
The Instrument of Change, 2014, p. 174

How often do you hear students ask versions of these questions: *Why do we need to know this? When will we ever use this? Will this be on the test?* Do you dismiss such remarks as typical student banter? Or do you lean in to the conversation, knowing that students have insights worth heeding when it comes to navigating their own learning?

As schools look to increase student motivation and engagement, decrease dropout rates, and cultivate more confident, creative thinkers, amplifying student voice emerges as an invaluable strategy. Although it might sound simple to turn up the volume on what students have to say, in practice this may mean challenging fundamental aspects of school culture. In this chapter, we will explore strategies to elevate the role of students in school change.

RECOGNIZING STUDENTS AS CHANGE AGENTS

I recall hearing Chris Lehmann, founding principal of Science Leadership Academy in Philadelphia, speaking on a panel at the annual International Society for Technology in Education (ISTE) conference. With two quick comments, he focused the discussion squarely on student voice. First, he asked the audience of educators how they reply when asked, "What do you teach?" The response he encourages among his faculty: "I teach students." Then, when another panelist brought up the perennial student question about relevance ("Why do we need to know this?"), Lehman advised educators to take that question seriously. "Students deserve an honest answer about what's worth knowing and why." He elaborates on this idea in *Building School 2.0* (Lehmann & Chase, 2015), arguing that the question of relevance can open the way to powerful learning:

> If we create our learning spaces as places where every student has the right to ask, "Why do I need to know this?"—where that is the first, most exciting question of every day—we can create vibrant, powerfully relevant classes that engage and empower everyone in them. (p. 121)

In schools that share this student-centered philosophy, students exercise their voice in the classroom, in school governance, and even in professional development for teachers. Science Leadership Academy students, for example, play an active role in organizing an annual conference called EduCon. They participate in everything from establishing each year's theme to selecting keynote speakers to facilitating sessions for teachers and school leaders who attend from across the United States.

Similarly, across the more than 150 schools that are part of the New Tech Network, students lead campus tours and speak with community groups about why and how education is changing. Starting in the elementary years, New Tech students become familiar with the concept of *agency,* or what it means to own your learning and advocate for your success. New Tech has developed a rubric for assessing agency, which is useful for framing conversations about self-directed learning with students and their parents (see Figure 5.1).

In their Aspirations work to improve schools around the world, Russell Quaglia and Mickey Corso have found that amplifying student voice unlocks a cascade of positive effects, from increasing engagement to building trust between youth and adults. What's more, they connect the dots between student voice and the acquisition of 21st century skills such as collaboration, communication, and creativity. As they explain,

> When teachers and the systems of school make collaboration between adults and young people an implicit part of their

Figure 5.1 This agency rubric is used across New Tech Network schools to frame conversations about self-directed learning. Having common definitions and indicators sets the stage for more productive discussions with students, parents, and teachers.

	EMERGING	E/D	DEVELOPING	D/P	PROFICIENT	P/A	ADVANCED
GROWTH MINDSET	• Is often hesitant to practice skills, even with encouragement • Is often hesitant to take risks in their learning, even with encouragement • Struggles to work through challenges without help or easily gives up • Struggles to identify strengths • Struggles to see failures and challenges as an opportunity for growth		• Shows a limited willingness to practice skills in order to get better at something • Takes limited risks in their learning or takes risks only with encouragement • Attempts to work through challenges but may easily give up • Struggles to build confidence from their strengths • Is beginning to see failures and challenges as an opportunity for growth		• Understands how practice and effort helps them to improve • Often takes risks in their learning (takes on challenges, goes beyond, etc.) • Works through challenges before asking for help • Builds confidence from their strengths • Sees failures and challenges as an opportunity for growth		In addition... • Actively works to improve skills through practice and effort • Independently reflects on their actions, decision-making, and learning (strengths, areas for growth, needs, etc.)
OWNERSHIP OVER LEARNING	• Is unable to complete tasks in a reasonable timeline • Struggles to see value in feedback offered • Struggles to complete tasks • Is often distracted and does not often participate in class discussions • Has not developed strategies for staying focused and on task • Is hesitant to begin work on tasks even after teacher or peer prompting • Struggles to build or maintain relationships and feels uncomfortable asking others for help		• Completes assignments at slower pace or alternative timeline • Understands the purpose of feedback and receives it courteously • Is able to complete tasks • Participates somewhat in class discussions • Has a limited number of strategies for staying focused and on task • Gets started fairly quickly on tasks after teacher prompt or direction • Maintains some relationships with others and asks a limited number of individuals for help		• Completes assignments and benchmarks on time • Accepts feedback and uses that feedback to improve their work • Is able to use a variety of strategies for tackling a task • Actively participates in class discussions and activities • Has developed a set of strategies for remaining focused and on task during work time • Gets started on tasks without prompting from the teacher • Builds positive relationships with others and feels comfortable asking others for help.		In addition... • Confidently seeks out resources and supports when needed in order to create higher quality work • Actively seeks feedback from others in order to revise their work • Monitors the effectiveness of strategies used for tackling a task and is able to adjust as needed

Source: Created with support from Stanford Center for Assessment, Learning, and Equity (SCALE) and based on similar rubrics from Envision Schools. © Copyright New Tech Network 2016.

everyday lives, then students are learning more than just how to get along with peers. They are learning about collaboration in "the real world" of the school and school decision making, not just in the more or less manufactured environment of a project. (2014, pp. 163–164)

Let's start by examining research about student voice. Then we'll explore a range of practical ideas to amplify student voice, from the classroom to the policy level.

WHAT HAPPENS TO STUDENT VOICE?

Most young learners start school full of curiosity and questions. Engagement is high in the elementary years. Yet it's the rare learner who still feels the same way by the time he or she reaches high school. The longer students spend in school, the less engaged they feel (Fullan & Donnelly, 2013). Their optimism, hope for the future, and creativity also decline with each passing school year (Gallup & Operation HOPE, 2013; Zhao, 2012). "The drop in student engagement for each year students are in school is our monumental, collective national failure," concludes Brandon Busteed, executive director of Gallup Education, the organization that tracks student attitudes (Busteed, 2013).

As they progress from the elementary years into high school, students are less and less apt to think that they have a voice in decision-making at school, according to student voice surveys conducted by the Quaglia Institute for Student Aspirations (www.qisa.org). Most students (63%) begin middle school believing they have a voice; the percentage drops to 36 percent by Grade 12 (QISA, 2014). The irony is not lost on Quaglia and Corso (2014), who state, "The more our students mature, the less opportunity they have to offer their opinions and participate as leaders in meaningful ways" (p. 2).

Turning around these dispiriting trends is not optional if schools are serious about preparing students for college, careers, and citizenship. Engaged students not only experience more academic success than their disengaged peers but also develop the tenacity to work through challenges and the confidence to generate original ideas. Creativity gurus Tom and David Kelley warn of the lasting damage of what they call *creativity scars*. At the right age, a single cutting remark can be enough to bring a person's creative pursuits to a standstill for life (Kelley & Kelley, 2013).

When we go to the source, students tell us that they hunger for authenticity. They want to make a connection between what they learn in class and what's happening the world outside of school. They are more engaged in school when they can see that what they are learning is critical to their current lives, their future, and their culture (Cooper, 2014).

Encouraging students to make choices about their learning contributes to intrinsic motivation (Brophy, 2013; Larmer, Mergendoller, & Boss, 2015). Not surprisingly, student voice and choice is considered a key component of high-quality project-based learning (PBL), according to the model developed by the Buck Institute for Education (Larmer et al., 2015). Without connecting learning to their inner drive to learn, students are apt to see school as something done "to" them. That's no way to build the mental muscles of self-directed learners and certainly no way to discover student insights that could lead to more engaging education.

TRY THIS: SURVEY YOUR STUDENTS

Knowing what moves and motivates your students can start with a simple question. To find out more about engagement, teacher and education blogger Heather Wolpert-Gawron surveyed 220 eighth graders in her language arts classes in Southern California. A recurring theme in their responses: relevance. As one student said, "What I think engages a student most is interactions with real-life dilemmas and an opportunity to learn how to solve them" (Wolpert-Gawron, 2015). How would your students respond to the question, What engages you? (Consider using these tech tools to conduct online surveys of your students: Google Forms, SurveyMonkey, PollEverywhere, Kahoot!)

How else can we encourage students to add their voice and valuable insights to discussions about the future of education? Let's start with an idea conceived by students themselves.

THE #STUVOICE MOVEMENT

Bringing students into conversations about school change is the goal of a student-led effort that has grown from a Twitter chat (#stuvoice) into a national movement. Student Voice founder Zak Malamed (@zakmal) was still in high school when he started #stuvoice to counter the adults-only conversations about education reform that he was following on social media (Malamed graduated from the University of Maryland in 2016). The grassroots effort has grown to include a national nonprofit called Student Voice (www.stuvoice.org), a Student Bill of Rights (www.sturights.org), and partnerships with adult allies eager to see students better prepared for college and careers.

A primary strategy of #stuvoice has been to invite students of diverse backgrounds and perspectives to share their stories about school. A national listening tour during the 2015–2016 school year focused on eliciting the stories "that you don't necessarily hear in student government," Malamed says.

Andrew Brennen, national field director for Student Voice, has facilitated discussions with students in diverse contexts, from Philadelphia to Iowa to Kentucky. "Students are a huge, untapped resource to help reimagine a model of school that's 100 years old," says Brennen, who took a break from his studies at the University of North Carolina to lead the listening tour. "Even schools that deliberately teach critical thinking," he adds, "teach students to think critically about everything at school except school itself."

When Brennen sits down with students for a roundtable discussion, he leads with an open-ended question: *What can you tell me about school that teachers and administrators don't know?* "The immediate response is almost always silence," he says, or sometimes nervous laughter. The first answers that bubble up tend to stay on the surface, such as complaints about school lunches or too much homework. Once students get past the easy answers, however, profound and sometimes heartbreaking stories emerge. Brennen has heard students share, "I know kids who go home and do drugs with their parents." Or, "I can tell you who's bringing knives to school because they're afraid." Concerns about bullying or harassment because of race, gender, or religion also emerge. On a more positive note, students say they welcome opportunities to make learning more personal. When it comes to project-based learning, Brennen says, "outcomes will be better if students buy in at the project design phase versus just at implementation."

The format for these Student Voice conversations mirrors an approach previously used to good effect in Kentucky. When Brennen was still a high school student there, he contributed to a successful effort to improve school financing. "We got together as a group of students and asked, What role can we play to help tell the story of what happens when you don't adequately fund education?" The Pritchard Committee for Academic Excellence, a statewide non-partisan advocacy group, invited students' insights by creating the Student Voice Commission. Students' yearlong efforts contributed to the largest reinvestment in education in the state's history. "We got a taste of what happens when we become active design agents rather than passive recipients of our education," Brennen says.

Student engagement in school change didn't stop there. Brennen and his peers conducted student voice audits in Kentucky, asking students to identify school issues they considered most important. In one middle school, for example, 230 of 800 students named bullying as the school problem they would fix if they could. In a companion survey of adults, not one teacher mentioned bullying as a concern. In another survey, students were asked to the respond to the statement, "I really want to learn." Among students, 80 percent agreed. Yet 70 percent of teachers in the same school disagreed that students were eager to learn. Those findings convinced Brennen that "there's a disconnect between how students experience school and how teachers experience school. It's hard to enact policies if you don't have a good understanding of everyone's perspectives."

For schools that want to facilitate their own student voice conversations, Brennen recommends having students take the lead as facilitators. "The roundtable is not a place for adults," he says. His advice: Rather than having adults select participants for initial conversations, invite diverse participation and welcome students whose voices are not typically heard. Make sure the stories that surface in listening sessions are documented and shared. And don't stop at listening. As Brennen says, "Students are used to being part of a system that marginalizes their voice. They get to the point where there's no interest in trying to change anything."

A variety of action steps can start to shift that paradigm. Let's consider a few.

DEFINE "THE WHY" TOGETHER

In their Aspirations work with schools, Quaglia and Corso have found that meaningful changes occur "when adults and students become partners and together lead the school in a direction that benefits all" (2014, p. 146).

Similarly, youth engagement expert Adam Fletcher cautions against school reform efforts that fail to consider what students think. "Students are rarely engaged in the processes that affect them most," he writes in *The Guide to Student Voice* (2014, p. 7). To counter this trend, Fletcher advocates for strategies to enlist students as partners in school change, recognizing that young people will not have all the answers.

"Giving students full control over schools is unrealistic and impractical. However, today adults generally act like students are incapable of leading and transforming education. Meaningful Student Involvement is the balance between students and adults throughout schools" (p. 19).

Previous chapters have described several examples of students helping to define "the why" of school change efforts. In Chesterfield County, Virginia, for example, students took an active role in the district's visioning work. They served alongside parents, teachers, and other community members on Innovation Teams, moving from ideas to action plans. Superintendent Marcus Newsome enlisted a focus group of students to provide him with feedback on key issues. Similarly, in Chapter 2 we heard school planner and architect Frank Locker outline practical strategies to engage students in focus groups during the visioning process.

To spark conversations about school change in the Salisbury (Pennsylvania) Township School District, the Innovate Salisbury team invited students to take part in an event called Question Week. Inspired by a shared reading of Warren Berger's *A More Beautiful Question* (Berger, Rugen, & Woodfin, 2014), Innovate Salisbury posed its own open-ended question: *What knowledge, skills, and dispositions do you think you will need as a graduate?* Chart paper was posted across campus to capture students' responses, which informed next steps in the visioning process.

ENGAGE STUDENTS IN "THE HOW"

When it comes to "the how" of school change, school systems are finding opportunities to turn up student voice in a variety of ways, from holding student-led conferences to enlisting students as partners in professional development. These are promising approaches, as we'll see in the following examples. But the most direct way to amplify student voice may be to foster more student-centered instruction. At the end of the chapter, we'll explore a range of practical ideas to make that shift in the classroom.

INVOLVING STUDENTS IN PROFESSIONAL DEVELOPMENT

Not long ago, I was getting ready to facilitate an all-day design thinking workshop with a team of high school teachers. In our planning conversations, I had asked my contact at the school to invite a few students to participate during the morning. That's when teachers would be engaged in the work of empathy: conducting interviews to gain insights from the student perspective. When I arrived for the event early on a Saturday morning, I found several students waiting at the door before any adults had arrived. They told me they were eager to see their teachers in a different role, as learners themselves. One girl confessed to being a little nervous. She had never been in a situation where teachers outnumbered students.

Once the workshop got underway, students offered invaluable perspectives about what interests them, both in school and out. Student interviews gave teachers new ways to think about everything from assessment (how to make assessment feel less punitive and more about learning from errors) to field trips (how to incorporate out-of-classroom experiences more often as a foundation of inquiry learning). After the students left, teachers kept coming back to their insights as they brainstormed and prototyped possible solutions. At the end of the day, I was surprised to find the same students hanging out by the school entrance. Curiosity had brought them back. I remember one student asking, "So is school going to get better now? Are there more questions you want to ask us? What happens next?"

Students are natural allies when it comes to school change efforts. That shouldn't be surprising, given the central role that school plays in their lives. Just as their insights are invaluable during visioning ("the why"), student perspectives offer a resource waiting to be tapped during professional learning to move change strategies forward ("the how").

Here are some examples:

- In schools introducing project-based learning, enlist students to provide feedback on project ideas at the planning stage to ensure greater student buy-in from Day 1. Better yet, survey them about their interests and concerns before designing projects, then look for opportunities to connect these topics to your curriculum.
- During projects, leverage student insights to troubleshoot PBL challenges. This is a familiar strategy at High Tech High, where teachers use a tuning protocol to discuss projects during the messy middle, not just at the end. Bringing students into those conversations can help to surface underlying challenges and elicit suggestions for improvement.
- During technology rollouts, tech-savvy students can provide essential support for both teachers and peers. Some schools recruit students to staff "genius bars," modeled after Apple stores, to troubleshoot tech questions and offer personalized instruction. Generation YES has published a guide, *The Genius*

Bar Goes to School, describing how schools can leverage student interest in technology to create student-run support systems for computers, software, and hardware (download PDF at www.genyes.org/files/staticcontent/downloads1.pdf).

In the Union R-XI School District west of St. Louis, Missouri, students have become regular contributors to professional development. Justin Tarte, director of teaching and learning, describes students as an energetic, no-cost resource that "we had sitting right in front of us" (Tarte, 2015, para. 4). The district began by recruiting high school juniors and seniors to participate in student think tanks. Students can earn elective credit for participating in research and development projects in collaboration with the district technology program. Students have evaluated and recommended STEM (science, technology, engineering, math) resources, for example, and then helped teachers learn to use new equipment purchased at their recommendation. Students in the district have also planned and facilitated professional development sessions for teachers, generating positive response.

A similar scenario unfolded with elementary students leading professional development at Cantiague Elementary School in Jericho, New York. Students offered to demonstrate a variety of apps that help them learn. That gave teachers a choice of tools to explore, as well as the role-reversing experience of learning from students. Principal Tony Sinanis was motivated to design the student-led experience after following #stuvoice conversations (Sinanis, 2015).

AMPLIFY STUDENT VOICE IN THE CLASSROOM

Teachers and school leaders who are determined to reengage learners are introducing strategies to reconnect students with their innate curiosity and build their confidence to ask questions that they care about answering. This is something every student deserves, and on an ongoing basis, argues Adam Fletcher. "Every student should have student-driven learning, Student-Adult Partnerships, peer-driven conflict resolution, and interactive learning conducted in school every day" (p. 36).

As you explore the following examples, consider which ideas might be a good fit for your classroom or campus. How might you modify or expand on an idea to fit your local context? How might you gauge the effectiveness of these strategies? How will you support students to help them become more self-directed learners?

Wonder walls and parking lots. Robyn Thiessen, an elementary teacher from Surrey Schools in British Columbia, Canada, wants to nurture and build on the curiosity that her young learners bring to school. That's why one corner of her classroom is designated as the "Wall of Wonder" (see Figure 5.2). Here, students post the questions that make them curious. These queries may lead to longer term investigations or Genius Hour research projects, or they may provoke a lively student discussion to start the day. Having the wall as a permanent artifact reminds students that the questions they ask are worthy of attention.

I frequently share the wonder wall idea with teachers who are interested in project-based learning. Inquiry is essential for high-quality PBL, and that means students need to be adept at asking good questions. If they have become accustomed to teachers asking most of the questions, they may struggle when prompted with the question, "What do you wonder about?"

Creating a culture of inquiry requires deliberate strategies. With older students—too cool for wonder walls—you might designate a graffiti wall or chalk talk space where they can post questions that

---

Figure 5.2 Wall of Wonder From Robyn Thiessen's Classroom in Surrey, British Columbia

Photo by Suzie Boss

intrigue them. Of course, you will want to establish norms for how the space will be used (and how it won't). A class hashtag can take inquiry onto social media platforms.

Teachers often ask the question, What happens if student questions go off on a tangent that seems disconnected from learning goals? Consider creating a "parking lot" for intriguing ideas that may not get addressed until a later date—perhaps in a different project or even in a future career. In a science class, for example, I noticed students using a corner of the whiteboard to record "hard questions awaiting our answers." (On their yet-to-discover list: How can we reverse climate change? What is dark matter? How can we prevent the loss of endangered species?)

Passion Projects and Genius Hour. Borrowing an idea from companies such as Google and FedEx, some schools are reserving

Figure 5.3   Terry Heick of TeachThought points out that Genius Hour gives students opportunities to determine not only what they learn, but how.

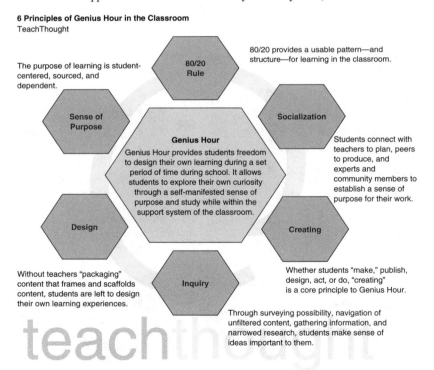

6 Principles of Genius Hour in the Classroom
TeachThought

The purpose of learning is student-centered, sourced, and dependent.

80/20 Rule

80/20 provides a usable pattern—and structure—for learning in the classroom.

Sense of Purpose

Socialization

Genius Hour
Genius Hour provides students freedom to design their own learning during a set period of time during school. It allows students to explore their own curiosity through a self-manifested sense of purpose and study while within the support system of the classroom.

Students connect with teachers to plan, peers to produce, and experts and community members to establish a sense of purpose for their work.

Design

Creating

Without teachers "packaging" content that frames and scaffolds content, students are left to design their own learning experiences.

Inquiry

Whether students "make," publish, design, act, or do, "creating" is a core principle to Genius Hour.

Through surveying possibility, navigation of unfiltered content, gathering information, and narrowed research, students make sense of ideas important to them.

Source: TeachThought, Terry Heick.

20 percent of class time for students to pursue projects driven entirely by their interests. Known by different names—Genius Hour, Passion Projects, iProjects—these are opportunities to step away from prescribed curriculum for at least part of the week and open breathing room for students to pursue their passions.

A key feature of such projects, which occur across grade levels, is the application of knowledge. Students typically make or produce something to show what they have learned or discovered and then share that with an audience. Another defining feature of such projects is student choice in *how* the learning unfolds (Heick, 2014). This means teachers need to be comfortable with students learning about different topics, at different speeds, and in different styles.

How do students respond to open-ended learning opportunities? One high school student told me that her 20 percent project provided a welcome mental refresher during an academically demanding school day. She used her self-directed time to pursue her budding interest in music technology. Another student said the invitation to propose his own projects fuels him through the rest of the school day, when he spends most of his time following teachers' directions.

Not every report is so glowing, of course. Students who are used to following the teacher's lead may struggle when asked to generate their own project ideas. Even top academic performers have been known to insist, "Just tell me what I need to do for an A." A middle school teacher I spoke with was surprised to find her students going to Google to search for "project ideas for Genius Hour," instead of tuning into their own interests. Such responses underscore the need for students to have more opportunities to be active participants in their own learning.

Curious homework. In a fresh twist on homework, students and parents in several corners of the globe are taking part in an initiative known as the Curiosity Project. This loosely structured inquiry experience involves students spending several weeks investigating a topic that makes them curious. For inspiration, they and their parents watch video interviews with people who are accomplished in a variety of fields (such as mountain climbing, veterinary science, or making art) and talk about how curious people get good at answering their own questions. To start the project, families use resources that the teachers behind the project have curated to set the stage for curiosity. "It's an opportunity to scaffold inquiry for a family," explains Scot Hoffman, the former elementary teacher who cofounded the popular project. The project also replaces the outdated weekly home-work packet with something more meaningful.

At the end of the experience, students talk about their discover-ies and reflections at a showcase event for the school community. Parents reflect, as well, about the benefits of kindling their children's curiosity (and the challenge of "not doing it for them").

GOING DEEPER WITH AUTHENTIC INQUIRY

The previous examples ignite student curiosity for at last part of the school day. In schools that emphasize authentic inquiry as a corner-stone of teaching and learning, student voice is persistent, carrying across the curriculum and throughout the school year.

At Science Leadership Academy, the Philadelphia high school mentioned earlier, students develop the skills of historians and storytellers by investigating the stories behind forgotten land-marks in their community. They use math and social science to analyze statistics about racial profiling by police. They excel as communicators and graphic artists when they construct museum exhibits in collaboration with scientists. Through project experi-ences that challenge them to make meaning by making a dif-ference, they make strong connections between what they are learning and why it matters.

SLA humanities teacher Joshua Block encourages student voice in both formal and informal ways. Insights and observations from students help him improve his craft and design more engaging learning experiences. Even if he's the one designing projects to meet specific learning goals, he gives students room to make choices and formulate their own research questions. Learning from—and with—students, he says, "is a way for teachers to deepen their practice, recharge themselves, and negotiate the complexity of teaching and learning" (Block, 2015).

I've heard many students say they "found their voice" through inquiry projects. A ninth grader at another school, for example, told he me wasn't so excited about learning when he began high school. Through an English project that challenged him to write about an unsung social hero in his community, he discovered what it means to take a stand for justice. He not only honed his writing skills but also discovered that he had a passion for public speaking. "This changed my life and opened my world," he told me.

To achieve such powerful results, projects need to spark students' interests and, perhaps, provoke them to investigate difficult questions. If students are used to passive learning, teachers may have to deliberately prime the pump for inquiry. Knowing how to formulate a good question—and having the courage to ask it—is a skill with profound social justice implications.

A protocol developed by the Right Question Institute ensures that every student has a say in posing questions to drive the learning experience. In response to a specific focus or prompt that the teacher offers—such as a photograph, other graphic, or short reading—students work in small groups as they follow these steps (Rothstein & Santana, 2011):

1. Ask as many questions as you can (individually).

2. Do not stop to judge, discuss, edit, or answer any question.

3. Write down every question exactly as it was asked.

4. Change any statements into questions.

This simple-sounding protocol has profound social justice implications. Dan Rothstein and Luz Santana, founders of the Right Question Institute and coauthors of *Make Just One Change: Teach Students to Ask Their Own Questions* (2011), first became interested in questioning techniques when they were working with parents in a low-income community. Parents told them they didn't participate in their children's education because they didn't know what to ask. That was more than 20 years ago. By now, Rothstein and Santana have taught question-formulation techniques everywhere from homeless shelters to adult literacy classes to community health centers. Patients take a more active role in their own care, it turns out, when they know how to ask doctors better questions. And people who have felt disenfranchised because of language barriers or low literacy levels can reengage as citizens by learning how to ask questions that matter to them. That includes students.

In project-based learning, the questioning process jump-starts the inquiry cycle. Instead of waiting for the teacher to assign research or readings, students who have generated their own questions are now poised to move their investigations forward. That doesn't mean students no longer require instruction. Far from it. Rather, the teacher's role changes from knowledge dispenser to learning facilitator. Teachers have the opportunity to teach not only content but also critical thinking and information literacy. They need to be asking questions such as these: Which sources are reliable? Is your argument or recommendation based on evidence we can trust?

Inquiry projects frequently extend learning beyond the classroom. Students may need to connect with content experts or gather information from the broader community. For teachers, this means being willing to learn alongside students rather than having every answer at the ready. It also means preparing students so that their time with experts is well spent.

In a project that involved schools from New York City and Atlanta, middle school students worked with consumer design professionals. Their goal: develop ideas for innovative school products designed for students, by students. A corporate partner sponsored the project and eventually manufactured and marketed the new product line, based on students' prototypes. Why was this project a good use of class time? Ailene Altman Mitchell, principal of Middle School 88 in Brooklyn, saw a natural alignment with learning goals, including creative thinking, problem solving, and collaboration. She also saw an opportunity for teachers to learn the design process themselves by welcoming experts into their classrooms. And because the project involved a real-world partner who would actually "take their ideas to the finish line," her students heard this powerful message: "Your ideas have impact" (Boss, 2015).

STUDENT VOICE IN ASSESSMENT

Assessment expert Rick Stiggins uses the metaphor of winning streaks and losing streaks to help us understand how assessment feels to students (Stiggins, 2007). For students who are used to "winning" at school, getting a good score on a test or paper reinforces their hopeful and optimistic view about learning. Students who are accustomed to "losing," on the other hand, start seeing every bit of feedback as more evidence that they just can't succeed in school. In both cases, assessment is something that happens *to* students. There's little room for student voice in assessments *of* learning.

As an alternative scenario, Stiggins encourages us to think about assessment *for* learning, with students and teachers as partners in the learning process. As he explains,

Assessment for learning begins when teachers share achievement targets with students, presenting those expectations in student-friendly language accompanied by examples of exemplary student work. Then, frequent self-assessments provide students (and teachers) with continual access to descriptive feedback in amounts they can manage effectively without being overwhelmed. Thus, students can chart their trajectory toward the transparent achievement targets their teachers have established. (2007, p. 23)

This approach to assessment is all about generating information that's useful to both teacher and student. Transparency takes the mystery out of the assessment process for students and helps them appreciate the value of critical feedback. Instead of giving students a single, final score for their academic effort, assessment for learning happens over an extended time and shapes the learning experience. It creates multiple opportunities to bring student voice into conversations about what's worth learning and for students to gain more information about their own progress.

"Student-engaged assessment changes the primary role of assessment from evaluating and ranking students to motivating them to learn," according to Berger et al. (2014, p. 5). By engaging students in the assessment process, these authors assert, students are more apt to understand the connections among attitude, effort, practice, and increased achievement.

During a project that emphasizes student voice, for example, students might set their own learning goals at the outset. They might collaborate with their peers and teacher to write a project rubric that will be used for summative assessment. They might reflect on their progress toward learning goals at multiple times during the project, giving the teacher a window into what they understand and where they need help. They might provide and receive peer feedback to improve their work at the draft stage. When they present their final work to an authentic audience, they may be called on to defend their thinking and reflect on their process for problem solving. Throughout the extended learning experience, students have a voice in assessment. They understand how critical feedback helps them achieve the learning goals that matter to them.

These are the kinds of experiences that help students become "leaders of their own learning," according to Berger and colleagues

(2014, p. 9), who are part of EL Education, a national network of schools that are part of the Deeper Learning Network.

Student-led conferences offer another powerful strategy to give students more voice in the assessment process. In these regularly scheduled meetings with families and teachers, students present samples of their work and reflect on their progress toward learning goals (Berger et al., 2014). Student-led conferences can be used from kindergarten through high school, as demonstrated by the network of EL Education schools across the United States. To work effectively, conferences require structure, a commitment by schools to create time, and clear communication with families. Teachers who are new to this practice will need time and professional development to get comfortable with student-led conferences. Students also need preparation time and support so that they have the confidence and skills to use their voice with a purpose (Berger et al., 2014).

COMING TO TERMS WITH STUDENT VOICE

If increasing student voice sounds like a worthwhile goal, how will you know you're achieving it? What are the indicators and outcomes of meaningful student participation in school change?

To get a better picture of how and why students participate in school, Adam Fletcher has developed a Ladder of Student Involvement (2014). Lower rungs on the ladder include activities that may treat students more as tokens or decorations than as real partners with adults. For example, adults may invite or even expect students to attend school planning events but then not encourage their input or action. At the highest rungs, everyone's unique abilities and insights are acknowledged and applied; students and adults are true partners in school improvement.

It takes ongoing effort to leverage student voice as an instrument for school change. "Student voice doesn't become powerful through some magical formula or mysterious bargain with students," Fletcher writes (2014, p. 17). Rather, schools that are successful at deepening student involvement do more than simply listen to what students have to say. They let students know that their input matters, and they encourage student action. That may involve training students in the skills they need for civic engagement or welcoming students into positions of authority.

At Sammamish (Washington) High School, where teachers have been leading a shift to PBL as we heard about earlier, student voice "permeates all levels of our work together, from students participating in small group classroom conversations to students partnering in curriculum design or establishing school norms and policy," reports science teacher Bill Palmer (Palmer, 2013). As we heard in Chapter 4, teachers and administrators have adopted PBL as a key instructional strategy to shift school culture toward more student-centered learning. They also recognize that students speak up in different ways and for different purposes.

The student body is the most diverse in the district, with 12 percent English learners and 46 percent of students qualifying for free and reduced lunch. At home, students speak 42 different languages. Nearly half the students will be the first in their families to graduate from college. Everyone gets a head start on college-level coursework by taking AP Human Geography in ninth grade. This emphasis on college readiness for all has resulted in a 15 percent increase in students passing at least one Advanced Placement exam and a 300 percent increase (from 20 to 68) in ELL students and students with disabilities enrolling in Advanced Placement STEM classes (Partnership for 21st Century Learning, 2015a).

The following continuum, developed at Sammamish, describes the range of ways that students express opinions, take ownership of their learning, and take action to effect change. Across all contexts, Palmer adds, there's a shared belief that "what students have to say matters in how learning happens" (2013).

TRY THIS: A STUDENT VOICE CONTINUUM

Use the Sammamish continuum (Figure 5.4) to generate conversation about student voice in your school community. Invite students, parents, teachers, and school leaders to respond to these indicators. How might you adapt this continuum for your context? How might you use it as a tool to encourage richer classroom discussion or guide classroom observations? How could it be useful in professional development?

WORTH ASKING

Although the previous examples of student-centered learning practices have been developed and fine-tuned by innovative educators (and, in many cases, have gained popularity through social media), not every teacher will be an early adopter, ready to take the plunge

Figure 5.4 Student Voice and Leadership Continuum, developed by Sammamish High School, Bellevue School District, Washington, outlines a school's progression toward authentic student empowerment.

Student Voice and Leadership Continuum

Integration (Teacher Led, Student Collaboration)	Transformation (Student Led)	Empowerment (Student Initiated and Led)
Teachers offer all students a variety of ways to engage (orally, in writing, in small groups, whole class, etc.). Teachers use a variety of methods (choice of activities/topics/assessment methods, surveys, focus groups, small/large group conversations) to regularly and intentionally engage all students in reflection about classroom norms, daily learning experiences, curricular units, and the classroom culture/environment. Teachers are transparent about ways in which they apply student feedback to their instruction.	**Teachers** provide a variety of means for student contributions and actively seek out and apply feedback from all students. They use student-generated questions to guide segments of the course, and give students practice with using tools to monitor their own and other's participation. Teachers use peer coaching and peer assessment in structured ways to draw on student voice and leadership in advancing course goals. Teachers intentionally seek out the voices of all students and are intentional in thinking about how they can flatten the power dynamics in their classrooms.	**Teachers and students** encourage and facilitate student leadership in their classrooms. They build student capacity for reflection, inquiry, and curiosity through the course of solving a problem.

Students actively ensure that all voices are heard when developing class norms and discussing content. They take responsibility for the learning of the community as a whole, actively seek out opportunities to assist peers inside and outside the classroom environment, and take initiative to provide feedback about classroom norms and culture. |
| **Students** contribute to the class through a variety of modes offered by the teacher. They see that their prior knowledge and backgrounds are a source of expertise for learning and classroom decision-making. Students are building their capacity to engage in discussion and collaboration about classroom based systems and how those systems can work best for them. | **Students** co-construct course content through formulating their own learning activities, questions and through regular opportunities for feedback.

Students take responsibility for successful conversations and discussions through initiating topics, making contributions without teacher prompting, and seeking out ideas from peers who have not yet participated. Students are empowered to raise issues with the class outside of teacher-designated times and are encouraged to use their own expertise and experiences to improve the culture of their classrooms. | **Students** see themselves as changemakers and key stakeholders in their education. They monitor their own learning and use that information to affect the trajectory of their learning within courses and the school.

School leaders create space for students to hold meaningful positions on schoolwide governance bodies and also encourage them to use their voice with school district and community decision-makers. Students are a part of building strategic vision for the school and also a part of responding to challenges, from truancy to plagiarism to increasing school spirit and pride. |

Source: Sammamish High School, Bellevue School District.

into activities or projects that amplify student voice. That means it's worth considering the following:

- How might your school or district do a better job of supporting teachers to increase student voice in learning? For example, could you offer greater choices in professional development or provide teachers with instructional coaching, collaboration time, or opportunities to visit their colleagues' classrooms?
- How do school leaders model and encourage these approaches? What more could they do?
- How might you communicate the value of student-driven learning for school visitors (for example, by enlisting students to lead and narrate classroom tours)?
- How might you engage stakeholders from your community as potential experts for student investigations?
- How are you preparing students with the skills and understanding they need to take action on issues that matter to them?

CASE STUDY: EMPOWERING STUDENTS AS SCHOOL DESIGNERS

If students could design their own high school from scratch, how would it differ from existing school models? How would they want the school culture to feel? What kind of instruction and assessment would help them learn? How about daily schedules? And could student voice remain central to decision-making once the school was up and running?

Students from Rhode Island have had the opportunity to not only think through those challenging questions but actually see their vision come to life in a public school setting. Students Design for Education, or SD4E, is a collaborative effort of the Business Innovation Factory, Rhode Island Department of Education, and Providence Public Schools, with funding support from the Carnegie Corporation's Opportunity by Design initiative.

Sam Seidel, director of the Student Experience Lab at the Business Innovation Factory in Providence, Rhode Island, worked with a committed group of student designers over several months to develop their vision for a new high school. Insights from the experience could help other communities engage their students in efforts to rethink education.

The process began with what Seidel calls "blue sky thinking." This was the students' time to dream big, ask hard questions, and not get weighed down with restrictions. Although students interacted with Seidel and other adult facilitators, they kept largely to themselves as they considered their wish lists for different aspects of school, including academics, staffing, culture, and physical environment. Video interviews captured students' early thinking (Business Innovation Factory, 2014). A student named Perla said she wanted high school to prepare her for "anything you want to do in life." Although students generally wanted to be able to "choose your path and learn how you want to learn," as another student put it, they also want school to offer structure and strong relationships with teachers. A student named Wesley cautioned against "too much freeway. That leads to slacking." His idea of an ideal teacher is "strict but fair, an old philosopher with a new face."

The research phase came next. Using a human-centered design process, students were challenged to investigate school from the user perspective. That meant stepping outside their own experiences to consider what their peers wanted from their high school education. "They realized they had a responsibility to others. They weren't designing for themselves but for their peers—and for students who would come after them," Seidel says.

Another aspect of research involved what Seidel calls "looking-out-into-the-world research." Students researched schools online, took field trips to see innovative school models that were close enough for a day trip, and used Skype to interview students and teachers at more distant schools. After synthesizing and reflecting on their research, they were ready to start designing their own model. "We met at night, on weekends, and for all-day design jams," Seidel says. Student designers were provided with materials to provoke questions and then make their thinking visible. For example, to prompt thinking about the school calendar, Seidel encouraged them to consider what could happen in 365 days of learning rather than the typical 180-day school year. "We tried to open everything up," he recalls, "and gave them tools and materials to provoke those questions."

Once students had developed initial design concepts, it was time for critique. Feedback came from a variety of stakeholders.

Adults who cared about the future of school for different reasons—as parents, educators, school leaders, and other community stakeholders—provided thoughtful critique. Student voices were also vocal during feedback sessions. Another group of students, from an organization called Youth in Action, served as a steering committee. They had done their own deep dive into educational equity and other issues and came prepared to give thoughtful critique. Their role was to hold the student design team accountable. "That meant there was another group of students providing checks and balances," Seidel says. They pushed the designers to answer questions and explain their model in detail. Seidel saw another benefit in this role for students. "At the end of the day, it was students who were signing off on the model. The design hadn't been co-opted by adults," he says.

Finally, it was time to put the model into action. When Providence Public Schools received a Carnegie grant to fund two new high schools, the opportunity opened to implement the student-designed model. Their suggestions emphasized mastery-based learning, strong school culture, and school governance that gave students power in decision-making.

"In a real-world way, students got to experience what actually starting a school entails," Seidel says. That included making compromises. For example, students had imagined locating their school in a brand-new facility. Instead, the district chose to have the new schools share space in existing buildings. One facility is nearly a century old with the boxy, brick architecture that student designers had hoped to avoid. "What students want isn't fancy," Seidel says. "It's like a modern workplace with lots of natural light, comfortable couches, and flexible spaces for collaboration. It's hard to do that in an old building."

When student designers realized their new-school model would be shoved into a traditional building, they were dejected. "That's when reality crashed down on the party," Seidel admits, "but that's what happens when you're forced to make compromises. You win some, you lose some." If students had done the planning only in the abstract, he adds, "it might have been fun but nothing would ever happen."

Another reality check occurred when there was a major turnover among leaders who had supported SD4E in the early stages. The commissioner of education who had promised to open a student-designed high school moved to another state. Both the mayor and Providence superintendent were newcomers. "We had worked to build relationships so we would have buy-in from all these leaders. But by the time the school opened, it was with entirely new leadership," Seidel relates. "We had to start over to engage them and make sure they knew there was a community that cared [about the months of school design work]."

Ironically, the student designers were not eligible to enroll in either of the new schools. The schools began with a first-year cohort of only ninth graders, with a plan to grow by a grade a year. The design team did get a chance to visit one of the schools, called 360, and talk with the first class of students. Designers were happy to hear that many of their ideas had survived implementation, especially around school governance and culture. "What seemed to stand out was that student voice was so strong," says Seidel.

What advice can other communities take away from the SD4E experiment? Seidel offers these reflections:

1. This takes real work over a long period of time. With student engagement efforts, you often seen students brought in for an afternoon to speak about their experiences. We kept the same group of students engaged over many months. They needed time to learn the jargon and understand the politics [of school change]. By engaging the same group with some longitude, they learn! They become knowledgeable and confident. That's key.

2. Having multiple bodies of students [the design team and the student steering committee] allowed for an interesting dynamic. They held each other accountable, peer to peer. They developed different areas of expertise and could offer informed critique.

3. Having a structured design process was useful. It created a path and journey for students to travel. That's different than just asking students, what do you want? We also took care in planning the experience so that we were respectful of students and their time. We gave them stipends and provided snacks. We varied the meeting places so that they got to experience some cool workplaces. They met interesting people and took field trips. We provided beautiful materials for them to work with. And as much as we could, we engaged in

storytelling and video capture about their work. That sends a message to them that what they're doing is important. We take it seriously, and others will benefit from it.

"If we really want to transform education," Seidel adds, "we need to be doing these kinds of projects all the time."

Takeaways and Next Steps

Students are an often-overlooked constituency in education change efforts, despite evidence that amplifying student voice can unlock a cascade of positive effects in schools. Rather than seeing themselves as active participants in their own education, students tend to discount their voice in school decision-making and to feel less engaged the longer they stay in school. Students themselves are campaigning to change this dynamic, as we have seen in the Student Voice example. Opportunities to increase student voice include engaging students in professional development, introducing more student-centered classroom practices, and giving students more of a voice in assessment. In the next chapter, we shift the focus to families and the new opportunities that are emerging for parent and family engagement.

CHAPTER 6

How will we engage families as partners in school change?

"There is no real reform without a permanent shift in culture, and part of that shift must be family engagement."
— Steven M. Constantino, *Engage Every Family,*
2016, p. 54

Strong ties between school and family produce multiple gains, well documented by decades of research. As classroom practices change, new roles are emerging for parent participation that go well beyond more traditional volunteering. When a school or district is heading into new territory, it's critical to include families in the journey. Whether it's a laptop rollout or the introduction of a teaching strategy to close the achievement gap, parents need to understand the reasons for approaches that may look different from how they "did" school themselves. In this chapter, we look at the many ways schools are reinforcing the important role of parents and other family members as active partners in their children's learning.

PARENTS AS PARTNERS

Parent involvement in school is associated with higher academic achievement for children, a finding that's consistent across demographic groups (Jeynes, 2005). When schools, families, and community groups work together to support learning, children tend to do better in school, stay in school longer, and generally like school more (Henderson & Mapp, 2002).

New instructional practices open avenues for parent participation in school. In schools that have adopted project-based learning (PBL), for example, parents often serve as content experts for student projects, provide critical feedback on student presentations, and gain insights into their children's strengths and passions through student-led conferences and from student reflections. Technology opens more avenues for school–parent engagement. For example, #ptchat is a weekly conversation among parents, teachers, and school leaders that takes place on Twitter. Social networks like Edmodo give parents a virtual window into what's happening in their students' classes.

Across the 150 schools in the New Tech Network, school leaders do extensive outreach to parent communities to make sure they understand "the why" of project-based learning and the thinking behind multifaceted progress reports that communicate more detailed information than traditional report cards. Conversations and open houses for families begin long before students are ever enrolled and continue throughout their school experience. The launch of each new project offers an opportunity to communicate with families about the learning ahead. Culminating events at the end of projects offer families the chance to hear their children reflect on what they have learned and why it matters.

Similarly, Jon Bergman, a pioneer of flipped learning, acknowledges the need to bring parents into the conversation when introducing such an unfamiliar strategy for instruction. Unless parents understand the theory and benefits of a practice such as flipped learning for their children, he cautions, they may wrongly conclude that the teacher just isn't teaching anymore (Bergman, 2014). Parents are likely to respond positively, however, if they understand that the flipped approach increases opportunities for individual attention and allows students to "rewind" a lesson and learn at their own pace. In addition, parents who may lack confidence or academic background to help with challenging homework can learn alongside their children by watching video assignments together. "You can learn how the teacher presents a topic, and you will be better equipped to help your son or daughter," Bergmann suggests.

To make the most of these opportunities, parents need to see themselves as full partners in their children's education, not spectators. To promote that message with families, P21 (Partnership for 21st Century Learning) and the national PTA (Parent–Teacher

Association) have teamed up to offer suggestions for supporting 21st century learning at home. Their suggestions for families (P21, 2015b) include talking with your children about global citizenship and how to be a responsible digital media consumer who can detect bias; and highlighting your own 21st century practices, such as how you collaborate with others at work or in volunteer or civic activities. Parents can support 21st century learning at school by staying connected with their children's teachers to understand instructional practices and by building their own digital literacy.

When Chesterfield County Public Schools was about to launch its 1:1 laptop program for middle schoolers, the district hosted a series of Camp Chromebook events for parents. "We knew that we had to have parent understanding of what a Chromebook could do to enhance teaching and learning," recalls Donna Dalton, chief academic officer for the district. Parents were invited to learn about Chromebooks the same way their children would—in hands-on learning experiences facilitated by instructional technology coaches and teachers. The free events, offered on several dates through the summer, filled almost as soon as they were advertised. "Our parents were hungry to find out how they could support their students in the learning," Dalton says.

How Families Engage

Parent and family involvement strategies vary from school to school, reflecting local traditions, demographics, and school governance practices. Across diverse contexts, however, schools that manage to engage families share three key strategies that are worth considering when it comes to school change efforts. They focus on building trusting, collaborative relationships among all stakeholders. They recognize, respect, and address families' needs. They embrace a philosophy of partnership and power sharing (Henderson & Mapp, 2002).

Some of the most compelling examples of school change, according to Henderson and Mapp (2002), involve low-income families who have organized to hold poorly performing schools accountable. Their efforts to promote equity are a powerful reminder that "all parents—regardless of income, education, or cultural background—are involved in their children's learning and want their children to do well" (p. 8).

Family engagement also looks different as students progress from elementary through secondary school. Michele Brooks (2016), former assistant superintendent of family and student engagement for Boston Public Schools, explains how parental roles change at different times in a child's life:

- In early childhood, parents carry their children, meaning they protect them and ensure they have a safe school experience.
- As the children transition to elementary school, the parents also transition into the role of a guide: They no longer carry their children, but instead walk in front of them, clearing a pathway to school and providing opportunities for them to learn and explore.
- In middle school, parents shift to walking beside their children instead of in front of them. In this position, the parents promote the children's independence and identity development while still guiding the children through school when necessary.
- By the time children reach high school, though, they take the lead from the parents, now walking in front and forging their own path. The parents' role is no longer that of a guide but rather of a supporter, advocate, and monitor. If children are struggling, the parents help them advocate for themselves and find and access resources, without stepping in front to take the lead.

In considering how to engage families as partners in school change, let's think about the many ways that families already connect with schools. Joyce Epstein, who heads the National Network of Partnership Schools at Johns Hopkins University, has identified six types of parental involvement (Henderson & Mapp, 2002). Each offers traditional activities as well as opportunities to engage parents in school change efforts. Table 6.1 describes the six types of involvement identified by Epstein (left column) and the school activities typically associated with it (middle column). In the right column, I suggest how parents might also engage to foster school change. These change efforts don't replace traditional roles for parents and families, but instead expand on them.

Table 6.1   From Family Involvement to Engagement for Change

Type of Involvement*	Traditional School Activities*	Engagement for Change
Parenting	Discussing children's interests, setting expectations (i.e., screen time), supervising homework	Encouraging children's curiosity and passions, modeling 21st century skills (such as collaboration or digital citizenship)
Communicating	Receiving school notices (newsletters, letters home, calendar updates)	Participating in book study, engaging in #ptchat (Twitter chat focused on specific topics of interest to parents and teachers), or using social media (i.e., Edmodo or Facebook) to gain insights into student learning
Supporting school	Volunteering, fund-raising, attending parent-teacher conferences	Contributing expertise to a project; providing an authentic audience or critique of student work; participating in student-led conferences
Learning at home	Planning enriching after-school activities, mentoring, supporting academic goals	Developing global awareness, technology fluency, sense of agency (for parents as well as children)
Decision-making	Serving in governance role (such as site council or parent organization such as PTA)	Serving on school visioning team
Collaborating with community	Taking active role in community	Leveraging personal network to connect students with real-life leaning opportunities

*Adapted from Henderson and Mapp, 2002.

Next, let's take a closer look at an innovative effort to bring parents to the table to think big about school change. Then, we'll consider strategies to engage parents who have traditionally been on the margins of school change conversations. Finally, we'll look at an effort to rebrand schools as more parent friendly.

Parents as Partners in R&D

Discussions about the future of education tend to emphasize the big picture, focusing on trends such as globalization, the explosion of information, and opportunities that technology affords for personalized learning. When parents join the conversation, however, the focus narrows. Discussions tend to get more personal.

The context that matters most to parents is "their own kid," says Shabbi Luthra, director of research and development at the American School of Bombay (ASB) in Mumbai, India. Whether parents are advocating for more openness, more relevance, or more flexibility in school, she adds, "they want education to be different *for their child*."

As part of its strategic efforts to innovate in education, ASB invites parents to actively participate in the work of research and development. The R&D department literally makes space at the table by inviting volunteers to take part in a yearlong parent R&D team. The team's agenda changes annually, based on the interests of members and issues facing the school, but the goal remains consistent: ensure that parents have a voice in school change.

Typically, the parent team kicks off the new school year with a shared reading to build background on a specific topic. In past years, for example, parents have read and discussed *Creating Innovators* (Wagner, 2012) and *Making Hope Happen* (Lopez, 2014). Parents also study trends and forecasting reports from groups such as Knowledge Works and the Horizon Report.

"We look at the trends together and ask parents, What does this mean for education? What does it mean for our school? That helps us move our thinking [as a school]," Luthra says. "It's not a condescending activity. We tell them, 'We really need your perspective. These are your kids. You are stakeholders in this.'" Parents who want a better understanding of teaching and learning at ASB are invited to take part in classroom observations, with an R&D team member along to help them debrief the experience.

"There's always a learning aspect to the work," explains Scot Hoffman, a former ASB teacher and now part of the school's R&D department. Parents aren't the only ones who benefit from these discussions. The school learns from hearing the ideas and diverse experiences that parents bring. "We end up in a different place than where we start," Hoffman says.

After building background about a particular topic, parents typically move into a design phase to solve a specific problem or propose a new idea. A few years ago, for example, the school was considering changing the master calendar. "Parents' ideas strongly influenced our thinking," Luthra says. Because most parents are coming from outside the system of school, they aren't locked into specific models. "They were far less conservative [than administrators and teachers]," she adds, when it came to rethinking the school calendar.

In another initiative, parent engagement helped to build momentum for the maker movement at ASB. Members of the school's R&D department were quick to recognize the potential of this global do-it-yourself trend to boost creativity, collaboration, and problem solving. After immersing themselves in readings and diving into hands-on experiences with tinkering and maker tools, R&D staff turned to the parent community to consider next steps. A parent R&D team came together to explore this question: What are the implications of the maker movement for our children? Parent involvement helped articulate the benefits of a "Maker Mindset" that would engage students, faculty, and parents.

To accelerate this idea, the school began hosting Maker Saturdays for parents and students to experience together. Consultant Gary Stager, coauthor of *Invent to Learn* (Martinez & Stager, 2013), was on hand to facilitate the initial events. Working and learning

Figure 6.1 Father and child team up to invent together during a Maker Saturday event at the American School of Bombay in Mumbai, India.

American School of Bombay

alongside their children, parents developed new skills and enthusiasm for learning by making. They tinkered with Arduino microcontrollers, LED lights, and low-tech materials. They learned the power of prototyping to make ideas visible and discussable. Some parents were so engaged, they set up makerspaces in their own homes.

"Then they pushed us," Luthra says. "Parents wanted to know why aren't we doing this more in classrooms?" That feedback helped to spark and sustain new initiatives that foster the Maker Mindset. In the middle school, for example, students take part in immersive, cross curricular experiences called Studio 6, in which they have four days to explore high-interest topics such as wearable technologies, movie making, or robotics. New high school electives enable students to learn primarily through design thinking, programming, and making (Luthra & Hoffman, 2015, p. 89).

In yet another effort to engage parents as partners in their children's learning, ASB promotes an initiative known as the Curiosity Project (discussed in the previous chapter as a strategy to increase student voice). The idea began as an alternative to traditional homework for the elementary grades. The Curiosity Project has expanded into upper grades and classroom settings as families have recognized the value of personalized learning. Hoffman, who prototyped the project when he was still in the classroom, wrote *Curiosity Projects,* published by ASB (Hoffman, 2015), to help both educators and parents understand the reasoning and research behind the idea. "Think about your children and your students. How often do their interests, intense curiosities, pangs of inspiration, or passions get to be the starting point of their learning?" (Hoffman, 2015, p. 9).

How might schools better engage parents who have not traditionally been active partners in their children's education? In some communities, the shift to digital learning opens new avenues for parent engagement.

ENGAGING THE DISENGAGED

When former superintendent Darryl Adams arrived in the Coachella Valley Unified School District in California in 2010, he realized that few of his students fit the description of "future ready." The high school graduation rate was stuck below 70 percent. Only 30 percent of graduates went to college, and among those who did, only 16 percent graduated. What's more, the agricultural community was on the wrong side of the digital divide. When he visited classes and talked with students, Adams realized, "None of these kids was truly connected" (Boss, 2016b). In the information age, he saw that disconnect from online resources and personal networks as a form of educational malpractice.

Adams understood that changing the game for Coachella Valley's 20,000 students would require a major community investment for infrastructure and tools, along with new pedagogies, digital resources, and professional development for teachers. He knew it was imperative for parents to share that vision and to understand "the why." One of his first steps was to run a pilot with 5,000 students to demonstrate 1:1 learning opportunities. "We needed parents to see for themselves that creating a 21st century learning environment would be a game-changer for their children," according to Adams.

Although poverty is pervasive in the Coachella Valley, where 68 percent of students are English learners and migrant families come and go with the growing seasons, parents had no trouble appreciating the need for digital fluency. "Our parents recognize that technology will be important in almost every job," the superintendent says. Leveraging parents' enthusiasm, he led the district on a successful campaign to raise $42 million in general obligation bonds to go from the 1:1 pilot to full implementation. It passed with a 67 percent yes vote, enabling the district to build state-of-the-art infrastructure, put iPads into the hands of every student from preK–12, and provide teachers with professional development to make the most of a digital curriculum.

A similar story has unfolded hundreds of miles away in Winters, California, a rural community of about 6,500 west of Sacramento. When Micah Studer arrived as assistant principal of Winters Middle School in 2014, one the first things he noticed was the tight bond between school and community. Families would show up en masse for games and other school events. "It's easy to see that the school is the heartbeat of this community," he says (Boss, 2016b). Despite that community support, the school was struggling with low student achievement, particularly among its high percentage of English learners. The school began a partnership with a program called Sch0012Home to address two concerns simultaneously: closing the achievement gap and closing the digital divide.

In both the Coachella Valley and Winters, parent engagement efforts have been key to technology integration and a shift to digital-age learning approaches. Indeed, in both communities, parents have been developing technology fluency right alongside their children.

At Winters Middle School, parents are required to participate in several hours of technology training before their children ever get their devices. That's part of the Sch0012Home model, which was developed specifically to help low-performing Title I middle schools and is funded by the California Emerging Technology Fund and The Children's Partnership. Parent classes in Winters start with equipment basics, then quickly move on to more advanced topics, such as how to check students' progress online, communicate with teachers, and encourage online safety and digital citizenship. Parent engagement has been key to program success, according to Agustin Urgiles, who directs Sch0012Home. "Once we get to 80 percent of parents trained," Urgiles says, "you see a transformation of the school culture" (Boss, 2016b).

Winters Middle School Principal John Barsotti decided that the goal of 80 percent parent engagement wasn't high enough. He set the bar at 100 percent to ensure that every child would have access to digital tools for learning. As part of the school's Chromebook rollout, Assistant Principal Studer arranged for parent classes on weekends and after school. The school provided child care to families that needed it and snacks for those who came hungry.

"Getting to that first 80 percent was easy," Studer says in hindsight. Even parents who had little previous experience using technology were quick to recognize the benefits for their children—and for themselves. "When children take these devices home, they can share with their families. That's how we can change communities," Studer says, by closing the digital divide that affects low-income families in both rural and urban areas. He was thrilled with the quick results, "but as our principal reminded me, the goal was 100 percent."

To engage the hardest-to-reach families, Studer and team "worked the phones like we were running a major political campaign." The outreach helped school leaders gain insights into family challenges. Sometimes the barrier turned out to be a scheduling issue for parents who were working two jobs to make ends meet. Sometimes it was a fear of unfamiliar technologies. Sometimes language concerns were the issue. "We started communicating almost everything in both English and Spanish," Studer says. "That tells our parents: You are a valued member of our school community. Your language is not a barrier to participation."

To reach the very last holdouts, Studer went to a community housing project and conducted tech lessons around kitchen tables. He says that experience taught him a lasting lesson about parent engagement: "It's not enough to open the door and invite parents in. You have to be willing to walk through the door yourself and go into the community."

Similarly, the rollout of devices in the Coachella Valley has opened new opportunities to connect with parents. "Everybody needed to be trained up," Adams says, including administrators, teachers, students, and parents. Weekend workshops gave parents the chance to ask questions and learn how to use digital tools to help their children strengthen academic skills. Emphasizing the importance of parent engagement for student success, the district has celebrated the Year of the Parent—more than once. "Every year needs to be the Year of the Parent," the superintendent says.

To keep parents engaged beyond the rollout, Adams has recruited a parent–superintendent advisory group from across the district. Each school has a teacher who serves as parent liaison. An open-door policy is intended to make all parents feel welcome, especially those who have not had regular contact with school in the past. Adams makes a point to reach out to parents "wherever they are, whenever they're available." That might mean visiting churches, attending community events, or even pitching in with a harvest if it gives him a chance to talk with parents. Workshops to build parents' technology fluency are offered in Spanish as well as English.

Parent engagement has helped the district troubleshoot challenges that could have derailed the digital transformation efforts. One early obstacle with the 1:1 rollout, for example, was the low rate of home Internet access. Some 30 percent of students lack high-speed connectivity at home. That means they can't use iPads to take advantage of online resources from home or even complete their homework.

When parents told the superintendent that they were driving their kids to school parking lots at night and on weekends to get on the district network, he had an inspiration: "I know we have many families living in mobile-home parks. I know we have school buses. Let's put Wi-Fi routers on the buses and park them at night in neighborhoods with no connectivity." Solar panels on the buses keep batteries charged to power these neighborhood hotspots. The idea was clever enough to earn a shout-out from President Obama during a White House summit of superintendents in 2015 and has been replicated by other districts.

Since Coachella Valley's digital transformation began, graduation rates have climbed from 65 percent (in 2011) to 82 percent (in 2015). The district has leveraged technology access to start a virtual academy and has expanded career and technical academies for high school students, focusing on high-interest fields such as aviation and robotics. The superintendent credits community collaboration as the key to the turnaround: "It takes everybody to effect change."

Worth Asking

The previous examples may have you thinking about engaging the hard-to-reach parents in your own community. It's worth asking these questions:

- What are the barriers that keep parents and other family members from engaging in their children's schools in your community? If you don't know, how could you find out?
- How can you "walk through the doors," as Micah Studer put it, and meet families in contexts where they are most comfortable and accessible?

How Family Friendly Is Your School?

In Boston Public Schools, former assistant superintendent Michele Brooks guided her district toward stronger family engagement. The district began with a theory of action that set clear goals for family engagement:

If BPS engages families in ways that teach parents how to support student learning at home, if we guide teachers on how to partner with families to make home an extension of school, and if school leaders establish a culture to foster these partnerships, then the school district will have families that are more meaningfully engaged and teachers that are confident about involving families in the classroom and school community in ways that impact student learning and school improvement. (Brooks, 2016, para. 5)

A number of actions have supported this goal, including a Parent University to build skills for supporting children's learning at home. Parents of third through fifth graders took part in the Parent Child Reading and Writing Club so they would have the skills to support their children's reading and writing at home. The district also awards a Family Friendly Schools Certification to schools that are exemplars at implementing family engagement strategies. The award recognizes school leaders for their family-friendly practices and provides some friendly competition. "This created a buzz around schools, prompting many to get more involved in family engagement in order to achieve the certification," Brooks reports (2016).

TRY THIS: FAMILY ENGAGEMENT DESIGN CHALLENGE

"How might we design a better way for families, educators, and community partners to support student learning—together?"

The invitation to explore that open-ended question attracted 120 parents, students, teachers, principals, and other community members to a weekend event in San Diego in 2015. Allison Rowland, doctoral resident in the Harvard Graduate School of Education's Doctor of Education Leadership program, facilitated the all-day experience for San Diego Unified School District. Design thinking provided the process for a diverse group—speaking at least five languages in addition to English—to engage all voices and generate innovative solutions by working together for the benefit of students.

Participants moved through a five-step design process, resulting in a slate of prototypes for future action. Describing the experience for the Harvard Family Research Project, Rowland emphasized the value of building empathy and taking care to listen closely. As she explains,

Typically, in Design Thinking, listening and building empathy involve conducting one-on-one user interviews. Because of limited translation services, we decided to flip the way translation usually happens: The families conversed in their own languages, and the educators listened to the translated conversation in English on headsets. We listened to families speaking Karen, Kizigua, Somali, Spanish, and Vietnamese. The experience was profound—many educators had not heard families' perspectives in such a direct way—families were empowered to speak to each other in their own languages. Educators and families reported the process built trust and often shifted their beliefs about each other. (2016, para. 8)

As a result of the event, an expanded commitment to family engagement is taking hold across the district. Rowland cites one example:

An area superintendent shared with us that she has seen a shift toward an "us with them" approach following the event, noting that families and educators are working together when a problem arises and asking how they can solve it together. It is no longer that one party is approaching the other with a problem and asking them to solve it. (2016, para. 11)

TAKEAWAYS AND NEXT STEPS

Family engagement strategies may look different from one community to the next, but the results are consistent. When parents and other family members are engaged as partners in their children's learning, everyone benefits. Changing instructional practices, such as PBL, flipped learning, or student-led conferences, open new opportunities for parents and other family members to participate in their children's education. To make the most of these opportunities, parents need to be part of the conversation about why school is changing and how those changes will benefit their children. Structured activities, such as book studies or R&D teams for parents, help to ensure that schools take advantage of parents' insights and ideas for school change. In the next chapter, the focus shifts to another important demographic group: community partners.

CHAPTER 7

Who else will join us?

"What we need is here."
—Poet Wendell Berry, "The Wild Geese"

Partnerships between school and community set the stage for learning to extend beyond the classroom. For students, partnerships can open up more of the real-world learning experiences that engage them, providing introductions to role models or access to resources. For both schools and potential allies, however, effective collaboration may mean thinking differently about the role of partnerships to extend learning from campus into community. This chapter examines strategies to build strong partnerships that serve everyone's best interests.

MANY SCENARIOS FOR COMMUNITY ENGAGEMENT

Some schools develop long-term partnerships with institutions or businesses that yield direct benefits for student learning. That's the case in Philadelphia, where students and teachers from Science Leadership Academy regularly engage with scientists and museum curators at the Franklin Institute. In other situations, short-term connections are formed for specific projects. In Metro Nashville Public Schools, for example, industry experts provide technical advice on student projects and consult with teachers about trends in fields such as automotive engineering and music recording. Elsewhere, it might be community members with deep insight into local problems who offer invaluable insights and act as sounding boards for potential solutions.

Despite the obvious benefits of community partnerships for student learning, these relationships do not happen automatically. Indeed, Kirtman and Fullan (2016) caution that too many school systems have adopted cumbersome processes for involving constituents. Endless rounds of meetings that never result in action are a setup for frustration rather than effective collaboration with stakeholders.

To disrupt that dynamic, Mount Vernon Presbyterian School in Atlanta has introduced new scenarios for community engagement. One is the Expert in Residence. Explains Head of School Brett Jacobsen, "This is not a traditional volunteer role. We're inviting people to let us call on them for their expertise." Experts respond to a range of requests throughout the school year. For example, upper school students might be showcasing their individual research projects (called iProjects) and want expert feedback. Or perhaps a teacher needs an expert to consult with students about a problem related to a specific discipline or profession. Having a community of experts ready and willing to engage means that the school can make connections quickly.

Another Mount Vernon event that has generated new partnerships is the school's annual Council on Innovation. The event is attended by industry experts who spend a day focusing on a specific design challenge related to education—for example, *How might we continue to prepare our students to be globally competitive?* Students facilitate discussions and prototyping sessions, using the design thinking process. Impressed by the students' facility with problem-solving strategies, one of the experts suggested to Jacobsen, "We should give you our problems [to solve]." Another proposed that students partner with experts on community problem solving as "reverse mentors." The school leader saw mutually beneficial outcomes, leading to student engagement on real projects with the Centers for Disease Control and Prevention, the National Association of Energy Services, and MODA (the Museum of Design Atlanta). In a recent collaboration, students worked with a real estate developer to design a small-scale pocket park to delight children visiting a commercial shopping center.

The examples in this chapter will guide you through questions worth considering when it comes to building effective partnerships in your community: What motivates business and nonprofits to share their expertise and valuable time with students? How can schools leverage assets in their communities to expand opportunities for students? How can educators ensure that internships or service opportunities that take place off campus actually connect to learning goals?

It's also worth considering when to say "no" to potential partners. Although forward-thinking school leaders welcome and seek out partnerships, they do not automatically jump at every opportunity. "We're not running a circus here," explained a principal from Brooklyn, New York, in explaining why it's important to evaluate potential partnerships to find the right fit and an alignment to learning goals (Boss, 2015).

Let's take a closer look at the strategies that are helping one partnership thrive and grow.

COMMUNITY AS CURRICULUM

We heard in Chapter 2 how the Iowa BIG high school model emerged from a stakeholder engagement strategy of sending adults back to school. Three years after launch, this break-the-mold school in Cedar Rapids is thriving with a focus on passion, projects, and community.

Troy Miller is director of strategic partnerships for Iowa BIG. "The new curriculum is community," he explains. "Our community has enough problems and opportunities for students to have an endless number of things to do." Miller serves as a conduit between motivated students and the organizations keen to have students grapple with their real-world issues.

Some projects begin with a student's passion or curiosity. Miller calls these "outbound" projects, such as a storytelling and photography site called Humans of Cedar Rapids (www.humansofcr.org). As he explains, "Outbound projects start with a student championing an idea and building a team [of fellow students] to join the effort." Not every outbound idea is a go. It has to offer substantial learning opportunities that connect to academic standards. If an idea meets that litmus test, Miller says, "then my role is to attach that team to a community partner."

"Inbound" projects, on the other hand, originate in the community. A business, nonprofit organization, or government agency identifies a challenge or issue for students to tackle. For example, students have worked with the city to develop and build systems to measure storm water quality at different locations. There's a vetting process to ensure that projects require students to be real problem solvers and critical thinkers, not just able bodies. Ideas that make the cut—offering the desired academic rigor—go into a "project pool" from which students make their selections.

When Iowa BIG was just getting off the ground, the teaching staff had to scout for project opportunities. That has changed. As word has gotten out about what students can accomplish, partners are stepping up. "Now we have organizations coming to us. We hold a Partner Palooza each year where organizations come in and pitch their project ideas to our students. They're recruiting us," Miller says. "The more we're in the community, the more this model propagates itself."

Trace Pickering, Iowa BIG cofounder, says project ideas began to multiply after one key meeting with business leaders. The Iowa BIG team explained its model and invited businesses to suggest projects that could benefit from an injection of student energy and passion. "The general response was, we love it but we're not sure we have the right project to give them," Pickering recalls. He realized that business leaders tend to focus on their top-priority projects. He prompted them to think about potential projects further down their wish lists, such as ideas that didn't make the cut when it came to resource allocation. "I said, don't give us the ones that are mission critical. What else is on your list that you don't have the resources for right now?" Pickering went on to explain his logic:

> If kids engage in the project and solve your problem, you win. If they try but don't succeed, you win. You'll learn what didn't work, and you won't have to repeat that mistake. Meanwhile, you'll be exposing kids to your industry and your issues. You'll be helping them learn.

Once he framed projects that way, Pickering says, ideas flooded in.

When a project is underway, Miller works closely with potential partners to set the stage for a smooth working relationship with Iowa BIG students and staff. He starts by clarifying expectations, responsibilities, and options. Some partners are comfortable working closely with youth; others prefer to be less directly involved. Miller has identified a range of options for community engagement, from sharing space or equipment to having students fully integrated into their organization. "Partners choose to which degree they want to work with students," Miller says.

Miller, who has been both teacher and entrepreneur during his career, understands that education and business don't always speak the same language. "He's the interpreter," says Pickering. "Partners tend to describe projects in adult language. They're not good at putting ideas into kid-friendly words." Miller makes that translation. He also knows how to present project ideas to teachers "so they can see connections to important, deep content," Pickering adds. Before diving in, all parties need to have a shared understanding of the project goals and expectations.

Because each project and partnership is unique, teachers have to be nimble when it comes to curriculum design. "The teacher's job is to build content and curriculum around the project, not the other way around," explains Pickering. "It's truly student first, curriculum second."

Over the course of a project, Iowa BIG teachers play an important role as intermediaries. "Teachers read the tea leaves," Miller says, helping both students and community partners navigate challenges and build successful working relationships. Partners may need coaching about how to listen to students' ideas and trust young people with real-world responsibilities; students may need to learn unfamiliar content or improve their communications or time management skills. Those are all opportunities for "the art of teaching," Miller says.

Short of launching a new school with partnerships at the center, what else can schools do to build strong connections with community allies? Next, let's take a look at two more narrowly defined projects that are opening opportunities for students, teachers, and partners.

FINDING COMMON GROUND IN CAMBRIDGE, MASSACHUSETTS

Cambridge, Massachusetts, is best known as the home of Harvard and MIT. Along with these world-class universities, the city also houses Cambridge Rindge and Latin High School, a public school serving a diverse population of about 2,000 students. Community partnerships have enabled the school to create extended learning opportunities for students and teachers alike.

One example is the Glocal Challenge, an annual event in which students generate ideas to make the world a better place, starting in their own community. Each year's Challenge focuses on a different topic that calls on 21st century skills, such as global citizenship or thinking critically and creatively about the future of energy. After several weeks of intensive work, teams compete in a pitch session to experts from the community. Winners then take their problem-solving skills onto the world stage at an international summit for high school leaders. Their teacher-advisers travel with them, taking part in professional development with colleagues from around the world.

The Glocal Challenge began as an after-school pilot through a partnership with EF Education First, a global education company with offices in Cambridge. The city of Cambridge came on board three years later, funding paid summer internships for Glocal Challenge teams so that students could have time and support to implement their ideas in their own community.

Figure 7.1 Students get familiar with brainstorming and other design thinking strategies as part of the Glocal Challenge. Winners from the local event attend a global youth leadership summit.

Photo by Suzie Boss

Principal Damon Smith describes the learning experience as "a high-wire act." He explains,

> It puts students in an intense opportunity to work on a global issue at the local level. This project forces students to learn a lot quickly, articulate their positions, and convince some heavy-hitters that their ideas have value. The more kids get those real-world experiences, the better.

Let's hear from the three partners about their motivations to engage in this project.

At EF's Cambridge offices overlooking the Charles River, Shawna Sullivan Marino is the point person for the Glocal Challenge. She has become a passionate advocate for the event, which accounts for only a small part of her corporate responsibilities (she is director of public affairs and community engagement for EF Education First). "Students grow up through the Glocal Challenge," she says. "They build confidence and learn to communicate in a professional way. They will take those skills with them as they go on to college, careers, and as citizens."

Developing the next generation of problem solvers is a familiar goal for EF, a privately held company. The company's founding family also sponsors the Hult Prize, a global social innovation competition for college and graduate students that culminates in a $1 million annual award. The Glocal Challenge is loosely modeled on the Hult Prize, but with significant differences. Postsecondary teams are older and more self-sufficient than Glocal Challenge competitors. Students still in high school may be just as eager as their older counterparts to tackle real-world challenges, but likely need more mentoring and instruction to be successful. High school also brings additional constraints of schedules, curriculum mandates, and limited teacher time. EF draws on its own staff to help fill the gaps, providing instruction in design thinking and access to content experts. Leveraging its extensive network, EF connects high schoolers with mentors. When it's time for their final pitch session, EF enlists expert judges and opens its doors to host the event in a formal corporate setting.

Over at city headquarters, Jennifer Lawrence coordinates the Glocal Challenge as part of her work as sustainability planner in the community development department. She became acquainted with the Glocal Challenge when EF recruited her as a judge. Later, she had the chance to travel with the winners to a high student leadership summit in Costa Rica that focused on environmental issues. That gave her a window into the 21st century learning that was happening through the experience. "I saw young people working together with youth from all around the country and the world," she says.

During the 2015–2016 school year, when the Glocal Challenge topic was the future of energy, Lawrence saw a natural alignment with the city's goals to reduce energy consumption. By offering paid summer internships, the city gave students the chance to put their energy-saving ideas into action. The experience helped students see what it takes to move an idea from the drawing board to the real world. Working alongside city staffers, students learned about due dates, deliverables, and real-world budgets.

From the city's perspective, the partnership offered an infusion of "fresh ideas and people power," says Lawrence. By piloting the students' energy-saving ideas, the city hoped to learn which ideas might be viable on a larger scale. The city also had another motivation to become a partner. According to Lawrence,

> When we do community engagement, we don't want to stop at lip service. We want it to mean something. We're big on walking the walk. This is a chance for us to show youth that their ideas are important. Their input matters. We think there will be a snowball effect of young people working on energy and climate issues as they move into college and careers.

At Cambridge Rindge and Latin, teachers who volunteer to be Glocal Challenge advisers have also become strong advocates for the project. Teacher Marya Wegman says the real-world learning experience "is the biggest and most holistic chance we have to do project-based learning. It allows students to make contributions to the world." In return, she adds, "our city gets to see the incredible things these kids are really capable of. That's rare" (Boss, 2016c).

During their summer internships in 2016, for example, 19 students worked on everything from marketing home energy efficiency kits for renters to conducting lighting audits and infrared tests on a city-owned building and recommending energy-saving improvements. "This data is very useful to the city," Lawrence says. "It's information the city wants, and students got to see that their suggestions matter."

Beyond the partners' commitment to shared goals, what else makes a collaboration like this one work? Here are some strategies that work in Cambridge—and should translate to other communities. Lawrence adds,

> Cambridge is just one town that's willing to take risks and try new partnerships. We're eager for other communities to see what works here and borrow our ideas. The same approach should work all across the United States, if partners have the will and desire to work together.

Clear roles. Schools, businesses, and city governments all have different goals, schedules, and daily processes for getting things done. Partners need to be clear about their division of roles and responsibilities.

"At the city, we don't know how to get field trip forms filled out or manage student attendance," Lawrence says. "That would take us a long time to figure out, but schools are good at those logistics." The school also handles scheduling, carving out time in the busy school day for teams to meet with advisers and mentors. City staffers, meanwhile, share their insights about how their bureaucracy works and what's required to keep a municipal project on track. EF leverages its strengths to coordinate the overall event, recruit mentors and judges, connect students and teachers to global travel opportunities, and reach out to other potential sponsors.

Principal Smith advises other schools considering community collaborations to make sure that all partners are equally committed. "This has been a true partnership," he says. "EF didn't just pitch the idea and hand it off to us. They have been with us every step of the way. We have developed personal relationships with their staff. The approach has always been, here's an idea. Let's work on it together."

Clear expectations. The Cambridge project brings together partners who don't normally connect, such as teens and municipal employees. Lawrence drew on her background in youth development to prepare mentors for their role. "For some of these students, this is their first job. I wanted mentors to know how to give positive reinforcement. What should they expect from a 14-year-old?" She also worked with youth interns to make sure they understood their responsibilities, such as being on time and using e-mail professionally. She found herself in the role of interpreter, coach, and, occasionally, troubleshooter to keep expectations clear. "If the mentors were frustrated, we would talk through it." A college intern helped students stay on top of logistical details, such as filling out time sheets. "It all takes time," Lawrence acknowledged at the end of the first summer program, "but next year will be so much easier."

Continuous improvement. Partners fine-tune the Glocal Challenge each year, based on feedback and observations from the previous year's event. This "always-in-beta" approach is consistent with the design thinking process that students learn as part of their experience. It's also a good strategy for maintaining communication among partners.

During the 2015–2016 school year, for example, Marino proposed moving the Glocal Challenge from after school into the regular school day. Her intent was to open up the Challenge to a more diverse group of students. "We didn't want students to have to choose between doing Glocal and their jobs, sports, or other after-school commitments," she explains. Making the change posed significant scheduling challenges from the school's perspective. Running the event during the regular school day meant making room for eight weeks of structured team meetings and design thinking sessions led by EF staff. Principal Smith recognized that the advantages outweighed the inconvenience. "What students gain from those [Glocal] meet-ups is just as important as what they're getting in regular classes," he says. He relied on his teachers to figure out the meeting schedule and made it clear to students that they would be responsible for making up any missed assignments from their regular classes. More than 200 students—a tenth of the school's enrollment—signed on for the experience.

The only challenge of continuous improvement, Smith adds, "is figuring out how you top the experience next year."

Learning in PLACE in Portland, Oregon

Catlin Gabel School is a preK–12 independent school located on a 67-acre wooded campus in suburban Portland, Oregon. It's a beautiful setting with a diverse student population—but also something of a bubble. Several years ago, the school began exploring opportunities to engage students more directly in the life of their city and build their capacities as leaders who can appreciate diverse perspectives.

The result is a collection of community-based programs called PLACE (People Leading Across City Environments), all focused on real-world learning with a social justice lens. Participating students come not only from Catlin Gabel but also from some two dozen schools across the metropolitan region. Offerings include urban studies electives during the regular school year, intensive summer projects, and youth-led community forums. Students' collaborative efforts have addressed everything from food insecurity to neighborhood walkability to city park design, with real clients on the receiving end of their well-researched efforts.

The story behind this innovative program illustrates the importance of patience and the benefits (and challenges) of community outreach for schools designing partnership approaches to teaching and learning.

George Zaninovich, director of PLACE programs, began on a small scale with a summer program in 2010. A sliding-fee scale ensured that diverse students would have access. He leveraged his background in urban planning and education to teach students "how to go through the research process, how to become an expert on a specific topic in short time, how to think." Students learned to use community engagement strategies and survey tools more often taught in graduate school than in high school. The quality of the early projects, all of which had real clients and meaningful products, attracted attention and an influx of students and clients from across the community.

In the summer of 2014, Tim Bazemore was brand new in his role as head of school at Catlin Gabel when he attended a PLACE presentation to a city planning bureau.

Students were presenting their research on how to improve traffic flow [on a high-capacity street]. Here were kids from all these different high schools presenting their research. They had done face-to-face interviews with business owners and pedestrians in a number of languages. They had researched demographics and growth patterns. When the audience of adults asked questions, the students responded so knowledgeably. It was pretty darn impressive!

Programming has evolved over the years, but every PLACE project builds on these three elements:

- Getting to know your community using a social equity lens: Students learn to investigate provocative questions, such as *Who does the city work for? Who's left out? How might you involve people who have not traditionally been involved?*
- Researching real-world projects for authentic clients: Students dig into issues for which clients need data or other information. Clients are typically nonprofit organizations or local government agencies.
- Leadership training: To work effectively on diverse teams with peers they may not know, students learn collaboration strategies to leverage everyone's strengths.

In 2016, PLACE found a new home in a gentrifying urban neighborhood across town from the Catlin Gabel campus. The storefront space—designed by students and called The CENTER—is shared by a coalition of educational institutions and nonprofit organizations committed to social justice and youth empowerment. Along with PLACE programs, offerings include after-school tutoring, help with college applications, and young writers' workshops. "Empowering youth to be engaged citizens is at the heart of everything we're doing," Zaninovich says.

Moving into this physical space involved months of outreach to potential community partners, not all of whom were receptive to an elite private school opening an outpost in an historically African American community. "We talked to business owners, church leaders, neighborhood activists, residents, politicians," Zaninovich recounts. "The process taught us that, for this to be successful, we had to give up a piece of ownership. When the community told us we needed a cogovernance model, we listened."

The coalition that grew out of those conversations includes six organizations, including Catlin Gabel, that run youth programs in The CENTER. The location is in a new building that is itself the result of a public–private partnership.

In hindsight, Bazemore can point to "being patient and listening" as keys to the program's success. "We took a year to work the neighborhood, meet people, be willing to hear 'no,' and not get angry or defensive. It's all about trust in the community and being genuine in our motives. Of course, we want to do good for our own students, but that's not the primary goal. This is about being *in* and *of* the community."

Meanwhile, back on the Catlin Gabel campus, Bazemore and his faculty have had to wrestle with scheduling, transportation, and other challenges that come with holding programs on another site. "We have to be flexible with some structures to support different kinds of learning," Bazemore says. He credits his faculty for their openness. "There's no grumbling over missed class time [when students attend PLACE programs]. No one's suggesting we move these to weekends. These are clearly academic experiences," he says, "and teachers recognize the learning value."

By late 2016, PLACE had engaged hundreds of Portland-area youth, who in turn had connected with more than 3,000 citizens from diverse backgrounds across the community. The program is poised to grow with grant support from the E. E. Ford Foundation awarded in late 2016.

WORTH ASKING

Shaun Tomaszewski, STEAM coordinator for Pittsburgh Public Schools, considers partnership brokering to be part of his responsibilities:

> I hear from community partners all the time that they want to support schools but experience roadblocks. They don't know how to get anything started. I hear from principals and individual teachers that they're too overburdened. They don't have time to enlist partners. I do have the time to talk with potential partners about how we could collaborate in a deep and meaningful way.

In this chapter, you have heard about several approaches to fostering school–community collaboration. As you consider these examples, ask yourself these questions:

- Who, within your school or community, might have the skill and finesse to be an effective translator for different stakeholder groups and might be willing to serve as point person for community partnerships?
- What would you hope to gain by developing new partnerships?
- What barriers are in the way of robust partnerships?

TAKEAWAYS AND WHAT'S NEXT

Partnerships between school and community can be win–win scenarios, but they don't happen without focused attention, effective communication, and clear roles for all parties. When the pieces do fall into place, students stand to gain from real-world learning experiences that answer their call for relevance. In the next section, "The What-Ifs," our focus shifts to overcoming challenges and building momentum for school change.

PART III

The What-Ifs

Only on paper do plans unfold without any pushback or detours. How do schools embarking on change initiatives maintain momentum and overcome resistance to "what-ifs" and "yeah, buts"? Let's learn from creative solutions that schools use to troubleshoot inevitable challenges, build on early wins, and respond to unexpected opportunities.

CHAPTER 8

How can we address challenges and build momentum?

"Perfecting the horse wagon won't get us to the moon."
—Yong Zhao, *World Class Learners*, 2012, p.162

Although collaborative visioning ("the why") and a focus on action ("the how") can set the stage for school transformation, success can be derailed by the details. Inflexible schedules, intractable policies, and initiative fatigue can all pose barriers to sustainable change. In this chapter, let's explore strategies that innovative leaders and school systems are implementing to keep change efforts moving forward. By anticipating the "what-ifs," building on early wins, and learning from setbacks, schools are better positioned to see promising ideas take hold and become part of the DNA of their communities.

HOW WILL WE KNOW WE'RE MAKING PROGRESS?

Schools can't afford to make change for the sake of change. Shifts in instructional practice, technology adoptions, or redesigned facilities need to yield better results for students. That's the bottom line that matters most to stakeholders, whether they are teachers, parents, school leaders, community partners, or students themselves. It's worth asking, then, how your school or school system defines *better*. What's the evidence you're looking for to show that an initiative is achieving positive results? How will you be transparent about identifying successes as well as setbacks? How will you keep stakeholders informed about progress toward the goals that they have helped to set?

In the classroom, educators ask similar questions about learning outcomes when they design inquiry projects. Starting with the end in mind ensures that they focus on what they want students to know or be able to do by the end of the project. Then they backwards-design projects with learning activities, checkpoints, and formative assessments to ensure that students reach intended learning goals. Throughout, students have a voice in their learning and ample feedback about their progress. When the same thinking is applied to a school change initiative, stakeholders are similarly engaged and informed throughout the process. They know the goal from the outset.

When Pittsburgh Public Schools launched a STEAM initiative, the district defined its "end in mind" by stating this theory of action:

If STEAM education in Pittsburgh Public Schools develops a Strong Curriculum, fosters and supports Innovative Teaching, and builds cultures grounded in a Collaborative Spirit, then we will enhance students' capacity to create their own futures. (Tomaszewski, 2015)

How will the district know if it is making progress toward this ambitious, student-centered goal? An accompanying rubric describes what progress looks like as schools move along a continuum from exploring to engaging to sustaining to systems change when it comes to STEAM education (see Figure 8.1).

For Shaun Tomaszewski, STEAM coordinator for Pittsburgh, the rubric offers a useful tool for helping schools evaluate their own progress. At the end of a year of working with teachers to introduce STEAM programming at one elementary school, for example, he facilitated a program review with principal and teachers. The results were surprising—in a good way. As he explains, "I was expecting them to be in the exploring to emerging region [of the rubric]. Instead, they're already moving from emerging to sustaining."

As evidence of their growth, staff could point to specifics, such as efforts to redesign their schedule so that teachers have more cross curricular planning time. They identified ways they are collaborating with community partners to expand students' access to STEAM experts and resources. Teachers also debriefed projects. When one of their first project-based learning (PBL) efforts didn't meet their expectations, they learned by analyzing the highs and lows of that

Figure 8.1 Logic Model for the STEAM Program at Pittsburgh Public Schools

	Exploring	Emerging	Sustaining	Systems Change	Proof Point
Strong Curriculum	Perform a curriculum audit of existing content and skill-based learning outcomes that are extant within current frameworks.	Work with educators to develop a sense of horizontal and vertical articulations across content areas and between grade levels aimed at optimizing student learning outcomes and eliminating disparities.	Curricular elements are refined in ways that facilitate the reflective analysis of student learning outcomes and how growth areas could be supported.	Faculty develop capacity and agency, in the on-going development of culturally relevant curricula, with the aid and support of content area experts and administrators.	Educators, students, and community members collaboratively enhance students' capacity to create their own futures.
Innovative Teaching	Research best practices and review case studies of successful STEAM education in large urban districts across the country that have eliminated achievement gaps.	Provide faculty and administrators with the opportunity to see what effective STEAM instructional practices look like, so that a shared experience and language can develop.	Establish forums wherein faculty and student voice can be used in making decisions around STEAM professional development and instructional resource needs.	Faculty work with one another in collaborative and reflective spaces wherein they establish personal and collective goals that optimize all students' learning outcomes.	
Collaborative Spirit	Explore potential partnerships with community groups. Develop competitions and showcases that allow students to exhibit their work.	Secure/deploy resources and content area expertise. Utilize resources effectively in an effort to facilitate formal and informal learning for students.	Assess the impact of on-going community relationship. Ensure that student learning maintains rigor and relevancy across formal and informal spaces.	Students across the District have equitable access to STEAM. Individual community members realize their stakeholder roles within the PPS community.	

Logic Model for the STEAM Program at Pittsburgh Public Schools. Rows represent points of leverage, and columns contain indicators of success that allow us to track progress.

Source: Pittsburgh Public Schools.

127

project. Then they applied what they had learned about PBL to plan what turned out to be a highly successful community action project in which students took a stand against violence. During the extended project, students applied their understanding of statistics to design and analyze demographic surveys. They integrated art and technology by screen printing banners and T-shirts that they designed. They practiced prototyping by developing a realistic plan and map for a community march and rally. Through the real-world learning experience, elementary students saw themselves as agents of change, equipped to shape the future that they imagine. In the teachers' reflections, Tomaszewski heard evidence of a transformational learning experience for students and teachers alike.

In a similar way, the New Tech Network has articulated what student progress looks like when it comes to nontraditional learning goals. What does it mean, for example, for students to develop a sense of agency? How can students, parents, and teachers chart the growth of an empowered, self-directed learner? To communicate what agency looks like, as well as the stages of growth along the way, the network uses a student agency rubric (see Figure 5.1, page 71).

Assessment tools like these take some of the squishiness out of school change efforts. Goals are carefully defined. Evidence of progress is described in commonly shared language that fosters growth. Not surprisingly, an application of evidence and research is one of the drivers of school transformation that P21 (Partnership for 21st Century Learning) has identified among its exemplar schools (Brown, n.d.)

WHAT'S ACCELERATING CHANGE?

From a policy perspective, Michael Fullan (2011) cautions school systems to be careful about choosing the right drivers to accelerate change. The wrong drivers—such as ad hoc policies that can cause initiative fatigue—can hold back or derail progress. Fullan recommends four drivers that develop new capacities and cultures in school systems:

- Capacity building, not negative accountability (which can stifle cultures of excellence)
- Teamwork, not individualistic strategies, so that the culture uses everyone's talents to obtain sustainable results
- Pedagogy, not technology, to shift instruction
- Systemic policies, not ad hoc policies, to avoid fragmentation

Katherine Smith Elementary, a neighborhood school in San Jose, California, has used all four drivers in its quest to reinvent education for students in a high-poverty community in the Evergreen School District. In 2012, the school's high suspension rate signaled to Principal Aaron Brengard a lack of student engagement (Brengard, 2015). To address the root causes of disengagement, he led his Title I school to adopt a more hopeful vision—focused on success in life rather than on standardized test scores. The new vision is shared on the district website:

Our Vision: Katherine Smith School will be the model of excellence for 21st century learning and community service.

Our Mission: Prepare each student to think, learn, work, communicate, collaborate, and contribute effectively now and throughout his or her life.

As staff considered strategies to bring this vision to life, they agreed to three core beliefs that have helped to reshape school culture (Brengard, 2015):

- We believe our students can and will achieve at high levels (every student is expected to be college bound).
- We operate in a collaborative, shared leadership model.
- We take risks and are innovative in our approach to meet the needs of our students.

Let's see how attention to Fullan's four drivers has helped Katherine Smith School continue to advance its bold vision.

Capacity building. To put students at the center of learning and develop their 21st century competencies, faculty began a shift to project-based learning as a core instructional strategy. A cohort of early-adopter teachers, along with the principal, developed a shared commitment to changing their practice after attending a summer PBL conference in 2012. That was followed with intensive professional development, facilitated by the Buck Institute for Education, to build teacher capacity with PBL. Not every teacher wanted to make this shift; staff turnover created opportunities to recruit teachers committed to PBL and comfortable with the no-excuses culture (Warrick, 2015).

Teamwork. Collaboration, one of the core competencies that students develop, is also practiced by staff. Every teacher belongs to one of three, cross grade leadership teams (culture, curriculum, and technology). As Brengard (2015) explains, "Teams monitor the focus, set the direction, deliver professional development and, when needed, advocate for further capacity building through consultants or additional resources."

Pedagogy. In tandem with the shift to PBL, the school has invested heavily in technology upgrades. Previously, tech was largely inaccessible to students. Now it's pervasive, with students also serving in tech leadership roles. Despite the expanded access to digital tools, technology is not used just for the sake of tech. It's thoughtfully integrated in support of learning goals.

Systemic policies. Katherine Smith School became one of the first elementary schools to join the New Tech Network, an alliance that has fostered systems thinking and connected the school with a network of allies.

Even with all four drivers in place, the school has faced challenges during its reinvention. An early issue was the tendency of teachers to "snap back" to more traditional instruction when the district introduced new benchmarks for student achievement. Brengard encouraged teachers to revisit their vision and build capacity through collaborative professional learning to go deeper with PBL. To avoid backsliding, Brengard (2015) says, "We stayed connected to our vision and stayed connected to one another."

We heard in earlier chapters about the research and development (R&D) program at the American School of Bombay. With each new initiative, the R&D team pays close attention to both accelerators and inhibitors. Let's take a closer look.

WHAT ACCELERATES R&D

Sustained innovation, rather than short-term tinkering around the edges of education, is the goal of the R&D program at the American School of Bombay (ASB). With each idea that it researches and prototypes, the R&D program keeps a close eye on specific accelerators to track progress and identify barriers (the accelerators are based on the work of organizational change expert John Kotter, author of *Accelerate*). By referencing these accelerators with every project it tackles, the school reinforces a common language to talk about—and track the progress of—change efforts.

For example, teachers and administrators identified as a challenge the learning loss that happens during school vacations. The "summer slide" challenge, well documented in research, is hardly unique to ASB. But because of the school's R&D approach, it became an opportunity for innovation. Let's consider how the accelerators have helped stakeholders engage with this challenge and monitor their progress toward addressing it (Luthra & Hoffman, 2015, pp. 77–80):

- **Accelerator 1: Focus on a high-impact opportunity.** Research on learning loss creates a sense of urgency within the ASB community and sparks the idea of an Intercessions program to offer students engaging, hands-on learning experiences during vacation periods.
- **Accelerator 2: Attract and maintain an Inquiring Coalition.** A planning team comes together to begin preliminary design work.
- **Accelerator 3: Envision impact and design a prototype.** Planning team develops a vision and action plan to set the stage for prototyping of Intercessions.
- **Accelerator 4: Attract volunteer inquirers.** Volunteer stakeholders step up to execute action plans, recruit instructors, identify possible partners, consider logistics, and gather feedback to refine the Intercessions prototype.
- **Accelerator 5: Remove barriers to inquiry.** During the prototyping phase, good communication helps to identify and address parent concerns, such as questions about transportation, meal plans, or weather contingencies, and turns potential barriers into program improvements.
- **Accelerator 6: Generate and celebrate early impacts.** Positive responses from parents and students are documented and shared (for example, via daily blog posts and a student-made film about Intercessions).
- **Accelerator 7: Keep learning from evidence and experience.** At this stage, after several rounds of prototyping, stakeholders develop plans for ongoing feedback and improvement for Intercessions.
- **Accelerator 8: Institute change.** A field-tested and refined Intercessions program moves from the margins to the mainstream, becoming part of the school culture.

Figure 8.2   Essential conditions for innovation power the accelerators in a model developed by American School of Bombay R&D Studio.

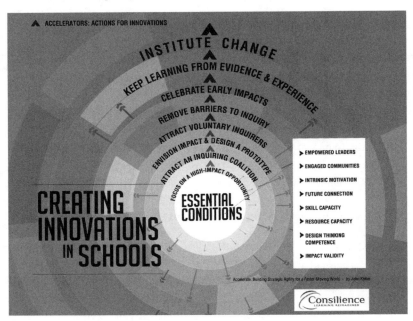

Source: American School of Bombay, reprinted with permission from *R&D Your School: How to Start, Grow & Sustain Your School's Innovation Engine.*

WORTH ASKING

As you think about the drivers of change recommended by Michael Fullan and the focus on accelerators at the American School of Bombay, ask yourself these questions:

- What are your accelerators for change?
- How do you track them and communicate progress to stakeholders?
- What helps your team avoid the "snap back" to more traditional teaching when you encounter new challenges/?

ANTICIPATE THE "YEAH, BUTS" AND "WHAT-IFS"

Change without challenge is an unrealistic expectation. That's especially true in education, where lasting change requires risk taking, learning from mistakes, and the investment of time and resources (Sheninger, 2016). Instead of expecting smooth sailing, savvy change leaders anticipate roadblocks and prepare to address pushback. They listen to stakeholders' legitimate concerns, but they're also ready to push through the predictable "yeah, buts" and "what-ifs."

Resistance is most likely to occur early in the change process, when stakeholders are evaluating their own readiness for disruption (Fullan, 2007; Murphy, 2016). That's when some individuals may be questioning their own competence, asking, *Do I have the knowledge and skills I need to go about teaching and learning in a different way? Am I up to the challenge?* Resistance can also come from challenging belief systems. If stakeholders haven't been part of defining "the why," they may doubt the need for change or feel reluctant to let go of traditions or practices they perceive as positive.

To tip the scales toward disruption, school change consultant Michael Murphy (2016) recommends three strategies, all of which depend on stakeholder engagement:

- Raise the level of dissatisfaction with the status quo.
- Strengthen the positive vision of what change will accomplish.
- Clarify first steps to make change manageable on an individual level.

Each of these strategies will be easier to implement if stakeholders have been part of the change process. Despite best efforts to get everyone on board, however, you may have some naysayers or resisters. Let's consider a few of the "yeah, buts" and "what-ifs" that a change effort may trigger:

- *Yeah, but we've tried this before.* Veteran educators have seen many an initiative come and go. Teachers who have lived through pendulum swings or short-term pilots can't be blamed for adopting an attitude of "this too shall pass." It's worth considering, then, what's different about the idea or approach you want to introduce now. For example, how are flexible learning spaces in your proposed remodel going to be better than the noisy and ultimately unsuccessful open classroom designs of the 1970s? How is digital-age PBL, designed for rigor and relevance, different from open-ended discovery learning of the past?

- *Yeah, but we don't have time for one more thing.* Lack of time is probably the most common excuse for not tackling change, according to leadership expert Eric Sheninger. He encourages the time-strapped to reflect on the big goals of education, starting with making a difference in the lives of children (2016, p. 57). In addition, collaborative planning should give stakeholders the opportunity to address concerns about schedules early, before implementation. And sometimes, it's smart to go slow. In Chesterfield County, Virginia, Superintendent Marcus Newsome built in a deliberate pause after several years of "putting pedal to the metal. Teachers needed time to breathe."

- *What if teachers (or students) aren't willing to take risks?* Schools that have made progress on innovation initiatives build on a culture that's tolerant of risk taking. For example, encouraging teachers to propose action research projects or offering small seed grants (perhaps funded by community partners) can encourage teachers to test-drive potentially disruptive approaches. Emphasizing *ungraded* formative assessment—and plenty of it—communicates to students the value of learning from feedback and revision. Leaders can also counter risk aversion by communicating plans to build capacity, such as embedded professional learning. These are all strategies that inspire confidence to tackle change.

- *What if parents push back?* We have heard several examples in the previous chapters of how schools have engaged parents in the change process from the start. That's one good strategy to build a groundswell of support, but it's not enough. Schools that are rethinking long-held traditions such as report cards, schedules, or even homework policies have to continue to communicate their purpose and be open to discussing parent concerns as they arise. At an elementary school that was ending the tradition of weekly homework packets, for example, parents were invited to discussions where teachers shared research about the limited benefits of homework in the early grades. The same topic was on the agenda again during parent conferences. To encourage informal learning and academic conversations at home, the school PTA began hosting family math nights and similar events to promote curiosity.

At schools that are part of the New Tech Network, parents are introduced early and often to assessments that don't look much like yesterday's report cards. Instead of giving students a single letter grade for each subject, New Tech schools describe students' individual progress toward key outcomes considered essential for their college and career readiness. These include agency (developing a growth mindset and taking ownership over learning), collaboration, oral and written communication, along with knowledge and thinking in specific domains such as math and scientific research. Pushback tends to dissipate once parents see how useful these reporting systems are for providing a more complete, multi-faceted description of student progress.

- *What if we're chasing too many trends?* Teachers who have seen initiatives come and go have learned to proceed with caution when they hear about "the next new thing." Leaders can counter skepticism by ensuring that any new initiative has clear goals to benefit learning and an evaluation system to track progress. Leaders who are strategic about change make a point of showing the connections between what may seem like separate initiatives. Schools that are introducing project-based learning, for example, may be also engaged in other initiatives around literacy, technology integration, or standards-based grading. Savvy school leaders help their staffs see the synergies of these initiatives rather than presenting them as competing agenda items.
- *What if change is too slow?* Patience is difficult, admits Eric Williams, a veteran superintendent who has led efforts toward transformational learning in two large districts. "But if you believe there is a big bang for the buck in the plan that you have crafted with your community, then you need to be all in on that" (Larmer, Mergendoller, Boss, 2015, p. 141). Being *all in* may require you to say "no" to other, potentially worthy ideas that would distract from the big goal or cause initiative overload.
- *Yeah, but it won't work here.* Some communities make a deliberate effort to scout for ideas elsewhere before trying to implement changes at home. For example, stakeholder groups might make learning journeys to visit different school models and then report back on their findings. This can be

a helpful strategy for driving community conversations—or it can backfire. Stakeholders may conclude that other communities have resources they don't or teachers more willing to take risks or parents less attached to traditional educational approaches. Cathy Lewis Long of the Sprout Fund in Pittsburgh encourages communities to start by taking stock of their own assets. "You can't take someone else's network and plunk it in your community. You have to build on your own strengths," she says.

- *Yeah, but colleges aren't ready for us to change.* Introducing a bold new idea, especially at the high school level, can set off alarm bells for parents and students who have been keeping their eye on college admissions. When Mount Vernon Presbyterian School introduced an optional Innovation Diploma for graduating seniors, Head of School Brett Jacobsen starting making the rounds of college admissions offices to explain the significance and the effort required of students to earn that honor. Similarly, the New Tech Network has had to translate its nontraditional reporting system, which tracks growth in student agency alongside more typical academic measures.

KEEP STAKEHOLDERS ENGAGED

Stakeholder engagement can be effective early on for catalyzing change, as we've heard in many of the previous examples. Keeping stakeholders engaged can help schools troubleshoot inevitable challenges during implementation and build on early results. Iowa BIG cofounder Trace Pickering knows that he can call on his community if he faces challenges:

> If we get a little pushback, we can point back to the documents that people created [which are archived on a website]. The school board feels empowered. It's easy to deal with any resistance because the community keeps telling us, go! They see that they're reaping the benefits. Iowa BIG is becoming part of the fabric of the community.

Similarly, as the Design for Learning initiative partners with communities to create new school models, a deliberate focus on change management strategies helps to keep projects moving forward and aligned with stakeholders' visions. Deliberate checkpoints ensure that districts stick with the collaboratively developed plans as they move into budgeting and construction. "The goal is for stakeholders to recognize their ideas in the final product," explains Ron Bogle of AAF.

It's also important to remember that new schools don't operate in isolation. "An individual school is part of an ecology," Bogle says. That includes the larger district and community. "You have to address system change [at the broader level] in order to have change take hold at the local site."

Genuine stakeholder engagement requires a willingness to disrupt the usual way that schools are designed and built. The typical approach after a bond measure passes is for the school board to put out a call for proposals, select an architect, and then start designing a school based on specs (such as number of seats or square footage). "Once you start down that path," Bogle cautions, "there's almost no way to do anything innovative. That is an administrative path that is largely focused on budget and schedule. It's essential but not sufficient," he says, if the goal is to build a nontraditional space that incorporates stakeholders' ideas about innovative teaching and learning. To break from tradition, district leadership "has to be unequivocally committed to being open to doing things differently. They have to communicate that without nuance to their constituents," he adds. If leaders are vague or ambiguous about goals, he cautions, "then bureaucracy will run the program. And bureaucracy will tend to do things the traditional way."

Earlier we heard about the collaborative process that led to the *Design for Excellence 2020* plan in Chesterfield County and a color-coding system to report on progress. Blue was the superintendent's color for ideas that hadn't been considered previously but deserved attention now. One such topic—student wellness—was raised by community members. They formed a Wellness Council with some 200 members from a wide range of backgrounds, from youth-serving organizations to mental health experts to nutritionists, along with students, teachers, and parents. "It was the largest committee I've ever worked with," says the district's chief academic officer, Donna Dalton. Wellness strategies that the council recommended were adopted by the school board, creating a new set of action plans for implementation and follow up. "We've had huge buy-in for this because it was completely from the ground up," Dalton says.

CELEBRATE SMALL WINS

Recognizing and celebrating early wins and small successes helps to build momentum and keep stakeholders energized. What's more, learning from prototypes can mitigate the risk of making big mistakes (Moran, 2015).

Superintendent Bart Rocco says his approach to school reinvention has been to "start small, then go like hell." He was inspired to introduce changes at the local high school after learning about the Entertainment Technology Center at Carnegie Mellon University in Pittsburgh, where graduate students do applied research in digital gaming, interactive storytelling, and other fields that combine technology and art. "We wondered if we could replicate that at the high school," Rocco recalls, to increase engagement and get students interested in cutting-edge careers. A cofounder of the innovative program at CMU told him, "If you can paint the walls, I can help you."

When high school students first saw the redesigned space on their campus—with couches instead of desks, brightly colored walls, and ready access to technology—some wondered if they had wandered into a new faculty lounge by mistake. The high school Gaming Academy, Rocco says, "has become a cool place for students to hang out and learn to build games and apps." From that modest start, the academy has grown into a four-year certificate program in gaming.

Building on that success, the district quickly introduced more innovation. For example, the Elizabeth Forward Media Center provides high school students with a suite of recording and editing tools. Based on research by Mimi Ito and modeled after YOUMedia in Chicago, the center has become "a place for students to hang out, mess around, geek out," the superintendent says. Elizabeth Forward has customized the media center concept, including a café run by special-needs students. "That's just as powerful as the other things happening in that space," Rocco says. Makerspaces have been introduced from elementary through high school, with age-appropriate tools and original curriculum to guide students' exploration of industrial arts and computer science. Along with expertise provided by partners, seed grants from the Sprout Fund, part of the Remake Learning Network, have helped cover the costs of prototypes.

The rapid pace of change in the district hasn't been without challenges. Not every staff member in the Elizabeth Forward district was eager to join the effort to boldly rethink school, and that has led to some turnover. "Some people will either ride with you or get off the bus," the superintendent acknowledges. To give teachers time to adjust to new approaches and new spaces for learning, the district encourages ongoing learning—for everyone. "We know that failure is an option," Rocco says. "But we try to send the message: *Don't worry. We'll learn from it.* That's exactly what we want adults to model for students."

By sharing its early wins, the district has telegraphed an eagerness to partner on promising projects. That attitude enabled the district to team up with researchers to introduce motion-capture technology and kinesthetic learning at the middle school. A specially outfitted classroom houses the school's SMALLab (for Situated Multimedia Arts Learning Laboratory; see Crib Sheet 402), the first such installation in a US public school. Here, students learn about math and language arts concepts by using whole-body motions and interactive floor tiles to maneuver game controllers. They also give critical feedback to game designers. "Our kids are learning and moving at the same time," Rocco says, "and they're also play testers."

With each new approach that's introduced, Rocco and his team pay attention to both hard data about academics and harder-to-quantify indicators of engagement, such as informal conversations with students. "If you're only measuring 20th century learning, then you're doing your children a disservice," the superintendent says. "What tells you that you are creating a culture where students are excited about learning?"

TRY THIS: LEARN FROM MISSTEPS

Just as important as celebrating early wins, schools embarking on change efforts need to be ready to acknowledge what's not working and learn from those results. A culture that welcomes risk taking and innovation uses prototyping to test ideas, make modifications, and evaluate results—positive as well as disappointing.

Although learning from failure is built into the culture of many of today's most successful companies, this remains an underused strategy in education. To shift the culture toward innovation, Zurich International School in Switzerland devoted a session of professional learning to a "failure fair." Teachers and school leaders shared examples of classroom activities or technology integration efforts that had not achieved desired results. In informal conversations, and with plenty of good humor to break the ice, colleagues debriefed the lessons learned. The importance of learning from failure was later reinforced by students themselves when they organized a TEDx event and invited speakers to discuss "The F Word." Not surprisingly, *failure*—and the opportunities to learn from setbacks—was a common theme for the all-day event attended by parents, teachers, students, and other community members.

Being transparent about what's working and what's not supports the development of an agile learning organization that can adapt to change. Many schools, for example, encourage action research to foster teacher-led change. However, it's important to realize that not every project will end in success. Sometimes, the best outcome of action research is an identification of practices that are not worth adopting and scaling. That's important data to share.

What does your school community do routinely to create a safe-to-fail culture and encourage learning from setbacks (by leaders, teachers, and students)?

TAKEAWAYS AND NEXT STEPS

Just as good instructional design starts with the end in mind, so do successful school change efforts. Clear goals, ongoing assessments of progress, and transparency about results are among the conditions that help initiatives thrive and keep stakeholders on board. In contrast, the wrong drivers can derail progress and lead to initiative fatigue. Effective change leaders anticipate roadblocks, listen to stakeholder concerns, use feedback to make improvements, and celebrate early wins. In the next section, we examine the importance of storytelling to drive change and help you plan next steps to engage your stakeholders in shaping the future of learning.

PART IV

The Future Story

A good story paints a compelling picture. When stakeholders hear stories about engaged learners and innovative teachers, they gain a better understanding of why the hard work of school change is worth doing. Social media tools enable educators to relay stories and scenes from the classroom, helping to build public understanding of 21st century learning. In this final section, we will learn about strategies used by effective storytellers and then plan the next steps toward your own future of learning.

CHAPTER 9

How will we share our story about the future of learning?

> "Administrators should be the lead storytellers of their school. Lead storytellers do not leave what is being said about the school to others. They choose what and how the story of their school community is told."
>
> —Silvia Tolisano, *Langwitches* blog

Storytelling is a strategic tool that effective leaders use to great advantage. As executive coach Howard Monarth explains, "A story can go where quantitative analysis is denied admission: our hearts. Data can persuade people, but it doesn't inspire them to act; to do that, you need to wrap your vision in a story" (Monarth, 2014). In this chapter, let's explore how to be more strategic about communicating school change efforts so that your stories reach the hearts of your allies, partners, and stakeholders.

LEVERAGING DIGITAL TOOLS

Increasingly, education leaders use digital tools and social spaces to bring to life their vision of 21st century learning with compelling examples from the classroom. Forward-thinking school leaders who are part of the connected educator movement use social media to highlight effective instruction and show what engaged learning looks like in action—by adults as well as students.

Figure 9.1   Eric Williams (@ewilliams65), superintendent of Loudon County Public Schools in Virginia, is a frequent poster on social media about transformative learning happening in his district.

Tweet from July 29, 2016.

Across Loudon County Public Schools (LCPS) in Virginia, community members receive regular updates about transformative shifts in teaching and learning from Superintendent Eric Williams, who is active on social media (see Figure 9.1). One of his first acts when he assumed the leadership role in 2014 was to facilitate a community-visioning process. Some 75 stakeholders—including business and nonprofit leaders, government officials, principals, teachers, students, and parents—came together for a series of forums to discuss this question: What does our ideal graduate look like?

From their resulting profile of a graduate, the district adopted an instructional framework intended to ensure that students develop those desired characteristics by the time they graduate. The framework incorporates best practices for project-based learning, technology integration, global citizenship, and the 4Cs of 21st century learning. To communicate those concepts succinctly and without jargon, the district has developed a model it calls One to the World (LCPS, 2015). It describes learning that incorporates four elements:

- Significant content and important competencies
- Authentic challenging problems in the world
- Public product for the world
- Connected with the world

Williams and others from the district often add the hashtag #OTTW when they post on Twitter about teaching and learning that is building desired competencies. Clear and consistent messaging keeps the focus on "the why," Williams says, and maintains the momentum that began with the visioning process. "It's important to stay in touch with our stakeholders about why we do what we do." When he tweets out about compelling projects—such as elementary students investigating soil erosion to protect their playground equipment, or middle schoolers creating a way station for migrating Monarch butterflies—he also shines a light on early adopters who can inspire other teachers to follow their lead.

At the building level, Aaron Brengard, principal at Katherine Smith School in San Jose, California, regularly shares examples of community problem solving, collaboration, and academic achievement that occur as a result of a schoolwide shift to project-based learning (PBL). He took part in #75daysofdata, a social media campaign in which he told the story of effective learning with a series of Twitter posts (see Figure 9.2).

Individual teachers, too, open windows on powerful learning experiences by blogging, tweeting, live streaming classroom events, and using other readily available publishing tools. Storytelling also happens in real time, when schools invite community members to take an active role in student learning. By making school change visible, educators who are pioneering innovative approaches tell the story of 21st century learning as it is unfolding.

Figure 9.2   From Aaron Brengard's (@brengard) Twitter series, #75daysofdata. Each daily post tells another story with a data point about engaged learning.

Tweet from August 6, 2016.

COMMUNICATING YOUR RAISON D'ÊTRE

Sharing your institution's vision on a school or district website is common practice in education. But words alone—or even a catchy logo—don't necessarily bring that vision to life or offer specifics of transformed instructional practice. To see how a school can leverage online platforms to make the case for school change, consider the example of a small, culturally diverse and highly innovative public school near Melbourne, Australia.

Wooranna Park Primary School, headed by longtime principal Ray Trotter, took its first bold steps into the future more than a decade ago when it began to redesign classrooms as immersive learning environments. Inspired by education futurist David Thornberg, these learning environments use digital tools and hands-on materials to fire up children's imagination and inspire them to embark on personalized learning adventures. For example, one space features a towering red dragon boat that students can guide using Google Earth or the Oceans view of Google Maps. Another area, known as the Enigma Portal, is outfitted with a green screen and digital tools that can be used for seemingly unlimited purposes, from Google Hangouts with content experts to collaboration on an international Minecraft project. Although these spaces may look and sound elaborate, the budget for transformation has been modest. Trotter and volunteers from the school community have done much of the redesign work themselves.

Physical features of the school represent only half the transformation. Teaching and learning practices have been reimagined to inspire inquiry and meet the individual needs of 350 diverse learners. On the day I visited, I saw students learning by making digital content, doing online research, printing 3-D prototypes, coding, and gaming. By fifth grade, students can earn the right to be "certified autonomous learners" if they can make the case that they are ready to drive more of their own learning. Teachers work collaboratively in learning communities to facilitate a differentiated, interdisciplinary curriculum. Teachers told me that they take an active role in school leadership and often design and lead professional development with their colleagues.

To explain the reasoning behind these many shifts away from traditional education, Wooranna Park has articulated its raison d'être—a set of core beliefs, backed by research and theory, that informs and guides ongoing school change (www.tinyurl.com/ncomem6). Videos on the school website illustrate the teaching and learning practices that unfold in this lively learning environment. All these materials are shared online, communicating the school's mission and methods to families, the broader community, and educators around the world looking for concrete examples of school change. Indeed, I first learned about Wooranna Park from two US education leaders who were impressed by the school's approach but had never visited in person. Virtual visits sometimes lead to collaboration between Wooranna Park and other schools or communities.

Worth Asking

As you consider the previous examples, ask yourself the following questions:

- How might you explain and illustrate your school's or district's raison d'être with specific examples of transformed teaching and learning?
- How do you use social media tools to help public audiences understand what effective learning looks like for today's students? Which storytelling tools should you add to your digital toolkit?
- How might you use storytelling to inform stakeholders about the research behind your pedagogy, invite partnerships with business or community groups, or recruit teachers who share your philosophy?

Documenting what happens in the classroom is an important part of storytelling, but what happens next with the documents? Let's listen to a connected educator describe three different uses of classroom artifacts.

Documenting by/for/of Learning

Global educator Silvia Tolisano, who writes the popular *Langwitches* blog about 21st century learning, encourages educators to be more strategic about sharing the processes and products of learning. Documenting what happens in the classroom is a smart move but doesn't go far enough to effect education change. As she explains,

Too often hundreds of images or long video recordings are taken, but nothing is ever done with them. Documentation OF learning turns into documentation FOR and AS learning when we DO something with the captured artifacts. (Tolisano, 2016)

Sharing classroom artifacts and insights via social media is a cornerstone of the connected educator movement. Colleagues who use digital tools to connect in personal learning networks (PLNs) gain anywhere–anytime access to resources, discussions, knowledge, leadership insights, and technology integration strategies (Sheninger, 2016).

"One of my passions is the globally connected piece [of education]," Tolisano explained in an interview. "I've been doing this for a long time. What initially motivated me [to document and share innovative classroom work with peers] is that I want to learn." Personal learning remains important to her, but Tolisano sees additional benefits if educators reflect on what they document and invite feedback from others. "This is how we can transform learning—connecting, getting authentic feedback, reflecting, sharing best practices. It's all embedded," she says.

To help educators envision the possibilities, Tolisano (2016) has developed a three-part framework that builds documentation into the learning process for both educators and students. In this model, everyone is a learner.

- Documentation OF learning asks a question: *What did we do?* It's typically a product or artifact of student learning.
- Documentation FOR learning invites reflection: *Where do we go from here?*
- Documentation AS learning encourages metacognition: *How are we learning?*

School leaders can leverage all three forms of documentation to share new stories about teaching and learning, invite collaboration, and help stakeholders understand the changes underway in education. As Tolisano (2015) suggests,

We live in a moment in history where change happens at lightning speed. Traditional pedagogy, tried and proven to be effective for decades, suddenly is proving to not prepare students with the necessary skills and literacies for their future. Every school, every administrator and every teacher is presented with opportunities for action research in any area of educational interest. By choosing to explore these opportunities further, we all are becoming pioneers redefining and transforming teaching and learning.

Perhaps you're wondering how you'll find time to add expert storytelling and documentation to your already full agenda. Let's learn how other educators have enlisted partners—including students—to help capture and share stories of transformed learning.

ENLIST STORYTELLING PARTNERS

A key strategy of the Remake Learning Network, discussed at length in previous chapters, has been to bring examples of reinvented teaching and learning into public view. Learning in the open happens in a variety of ways, from public showcases to open-source publishing. The Sprout Fund, a nonprofit partner that has helped to grow and sustain the network, is strategic about telling the story of education change across the region. Stories not only make change visible but often capture the earliest evidence of shifts in education.

Cathy Lewis Long, CEO of the Sprout Fund, explains that both quantitative and qualitative measures are important to show impact of groundbreaking work. Longitudinal studies are essential, but stories tend to emerge more quickly than hard data. "As a catalytic funder, you're the most upstream of an idea. It can be hard to show impact with projects that don't bear fruit until later," she says. Meanwhile, the organizations that are designing and implementing innovative programs may lack the time or resources to stop and tell their own stories. "Taking high-quality video or sharing out a story are things that some partners may not be equipped to do well," she acknowledges.

The Sprout Fund has helped to fill the storytelling gap by producing videos and publishing resources such as the open-source *Playbook* that captures emerging practices for teaching and learning along with network-building strategies. The organization also has formed alliances with public media partners that produce original content on the theme of learning innovation. Instead of hearing occasional, one-off stories about novel programs, the community gets a steady media diet about educational innovation across the region. "It would be hard for individual stories to harness the same attention and awareness," Long suspects.

To see how Remake Learning uses storytelling to build community support for new ideas, consider how the network developed and introduced the concept of digital badges (sometimes called microcredentials). Badges recognize the competencies that learners develop through their pursuit of hobbies and interests, both in and out of school. To launch a badging initiative, the network planned a series of community engagement events, each with an emphasis on creating and collecting stories (Remake Learning, 2015):

- A two-hour kickoff, attended by 150 people, launched the initiative. The public event included presentations by nationally recognized leaders in connected learning and microcredentialing. This built common understanding and excitement for the idea of badging, included time for networking, and sparked participants' interest in contributing to next steps by joining working groups.
- A series of awareness-building events engaged the broader community in talking about digital badges and learning pathways. Each event focused on a different topic and featured a guest speaker (such as a learning scientist or local organization that had developed badges for summer learning).
- A well-attended town hall meeting offered a large audience of teachers, students, mentors, and others to explore ways to connect in-school and out-of-school learning experiences across the region. This event (attended by 300 adults and 100 students) did not happen by accident. Careful planning resulted in a range of activities, including remarks from the stage, multimedia presentations, panel discussions, table-based facilitation activities, science fair–style feedback stations, Ignite Talks, and an enthusiastic emcee. To keep the all-day event moving, no one person had the stage for longer than 15 minutes. Throughout the day, diverse participants shared their reflections—about learning and life—at a "storytelling station" staffed by a videography team.

To help others learn from its experience, the network documented its entire process on a Remake Learning Competencies website (www.remakelearning.org/competencies).

Figure 9.3 Digital badges, including this set to recognize technical competencies in coding and gaming, were developed through a collaborative process by Remake Learning in Pittsburgh, Pennsylvania.

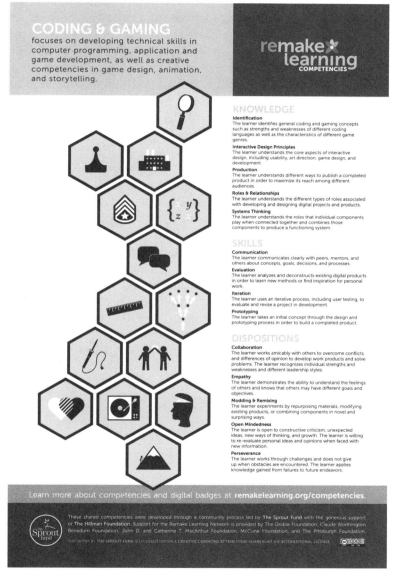

Source: The Sprout Fund. Coding and Gaming Competencies (http://downloads.sproutfund .org/remakelearning/competencies/posters/RemakeLearning_Competencies_Coding-Gaming .pdf). Creative Commons Attribution 4.0 International (CC BY 4.0) (https://creativecommons .org/licenses/by/4.0/).

ENGAGE STUDENT AMBASSADORS

In communities that are reimagining school, students may be the best ambassadors for 21st century learning. They can take their experiences into the community by serving as guest speakers at public events or guiding tours of learning in action. This is a routine role for students in many schools across the Deeper Learning Network. Leading by example, students make a convincing case for nurturing learners who can communicate, collaborate, think critically, and solve problems creatively.

Public events that showcase student work offer another strategy to make learning visible. Metro Nashville Public Schools, for example, hosts an annual exhibition of projects from across the district. This is a chance for community members to go to the source and talk with hundreds of students about their learning experiences. Throughout the year, the district collaborates extensively with community partners who team up with teachers to plan projects that reflect industry trends. The exhibition lets partners see the results of their collaboration and also critique student work.

Planning an exhibition of learning takes time and effort but offers lasting benefits. For Katherine Smith Elementary School, described earlier, the first public exhibition of projects unleashed a groundswell of community support for the transformation to project-based learning. Some 1,500 community members packed the 50-year-old school building to talk with students about their 21st century learning experiences.

WORTH ASKING

As you consider the importance of storytelling to achieve the changes that you hope to see, ask yourself these questions:

- Who are the expert storytellers in your school system or community? How might you enlist them as partners to shape your story?
- Are you leveraging the voices and talents of students to shape and share your story of learning?
- How might you overcome obstacles such as limited staff time or resources to devote to organizing an exhibition of learning?

TAKEAWAYS AND NEXT STEPS

Storytelling is an important part of the change process and deserves ongoing attention. Stories that paint a picture of the future of learning help audiences recognize the need for school change and celebrate the evidence of progress toward shared goals. Digital tools can be useful for conveying classroom scenes to wide audiences, painting a picture of learning in action. Expert storytelling partners, including students, can share in the task of capturing and crafting stories of successful teaching and learning. In the next chapter, we revisit some big questions to help you plan your next steps.

CHAPTER 10

What are your next steps?

"Change starts when someone sees the next step."
—Bill Drayton, founder of Ashoka

After a few years of leading his school toward a new vision aligned with 21st century goals, head of Mount Vernon Presbyterian School Brett Jacobsen visited a kindergarten class. He asked students to tell him what they were learning. What were they working on that was exciting? Without hesitation, students clamored to tell him about a design challenge that they were tackling with a class of fourth graders to improve their outdoor playground. As these five- and six-year-olds described their process, it was clear that they were already fluent in the language of innovation. They understood that good questions would lead them to answers. They knew how to collaborate. They realized that they had the power to generate original ideas and put them into action. The school leader paused to reflect on what he was hearing and asked himself, "Wow, are we going to be ready for these kindergartners?"

As educators prepare students for the uncertain challenges ahead, they have to think of themselves as futurists. That's a role that Jacobsen and other forward-thinking school leaders have come to embrace. Preparing students for what's ahead is embedded in initiatives such as Future Ready Schools and the Deeper Learning Network. Although no one can predict exactly how the world will change for our students, we know they need opportunities now to become more agile, adaptable learners and more confident, creative problem solvers. As they develop these competencies, we also need to make sure that school keeps pace so that it remains relevant and engaging for them.

What's the path that will take you and your stakeholders into that future? What actions are you considering to ignite or accelerate change to better engage and prepare your students for what's ahead? In this closing chapter, let's revisit the big questions that we have explored throughout this book. Ask yourself these questions: Which strategies that we've explored offer the best fit for your community? Why? What are you ready to tackle first? Who's with you on your journey? Your answers will provide you with the outline of an action plan.

ARE YOU READY FOR DISRUPTION?

In the previous chapters, you have heard about school systems adopting a variety of pedagogies and practices (sometimes in combination) that have the potential to transform teaching and learning. In the many examples and case studies that you have explored, schools have been strategic about introducing new initiatives to help them achieve their vision. They haven't pursued change for the sake of change or overwhelmed their staffs with short-term initiatives.

Take another look at the Crib Sheet 101 (p. 4). Then rate your current use and comfort level with each of the following. Better yet, do this with a group of stakeholders and come to a consensus about results.

Potentially Disruptive Practice	Current Use	Comfort Level
	How often do you see this practice in your school or across your system? Rate from 1 star (never see it) to 5 stars (widely adopted).	Rate your comfort level with this practice from 1 star (not gonna happen) to 5 stars (on everybody's wish list).
Blended learning		
Connected learning		
Deeper learning		
Design thinking		
4Cs		
Flipped learning		
Genius Hour		
Global education		
Maker education		
Personalized learning		
Project-based learning		

Based on your assessment, which practice (or combination of practices) seems like the next best thing for your school or district? How would this practice benefit students? How would the introduction of this practice help your school or district make progress toward your shared vision? How well would it align with other initiatives?

Now consider potential catalysts to drive change in your community. What's generating conversation about these topics among your stakeholders? Can you point to news coverage, safety incidents, or other events that have raised concerns? Which stakeholder groups are most vocal? Think about how you might leverage these catalysts to build buy-in for the practices that you want to pursue.

- **Rigor, readiness, and equity.** Are graduation rates or the achievement gap of particular concern in your community? How about college readiness of your high school graduates? How are more rigorous standards driving conversations about the need for different approaches to instruction to meet the needs of all learners?
- **Technology integration.** Is your community considering a technology rollout or investment in infrastructure to improve online access? How do you expect that teaching and learning will change as a result of increased technology access?

- **Facility makeovers.** Do you have aging school facilities? Are there deferred maintenance or safety concerns that are generating conversations in your community? How might you shift the focus of those conversations so that you start with learning goals before designing facilities to support those goals?
- **Design thinking.** Have stakeholders had previous experience or training in design thinking as a process for collaborative problem solving? How might you bring this expertise into discussions about school change?
- **External pressures.** Is your community experiencing a change in population patterns (such as in-migration or brain drain of young adults)? How about economic changes? How might external pressures (such as a brain drain or change in local employment opportunities) motivate community members to focus on school goals?

How Will You Engage the Willing?

You've heard about a wide range of strategies to ignite conversation and enlist (or convince) stakeholders to support school change efforts. Now's the time to think about potential allies in your community.

Build your network. Who are your most engaged stakeholders already? Who else might they bring into a conversation about school change. (For example: Parents are most engaged; they might bring coworkers or employers.)

Find a convener. Is there a local organization that might serve as convener of a big conversation about school change? This might be a media organization (as in Iowa), foundation (as in Pittsburgh), local employer, or nonprofit focused on community development or social justice.

Catalyze conversation. Consider the communication catalysts discussed earlier. Which of these might bring people together in your community? Think about strategies to encourage broader participation, such as providing child care or snacks, offering transportation, advertising via social media, or holding events in nonschool venues (such as workplaces or libraries) and at varied times. One district piggybacked on other community gatherings, such as fairs and sporting events, to connect with busy adults. Other opportunities for community conversations might include the following:

- Film screening with panel discussion
- Book study for parents, teachers, and other community groups
- Shadow a student
- Social media conversations
- Profile of a graduate conversation
- Other community events

HOW WILL SCHOOL LEADERS TAKE CHARGE OF CHANGE?

What is your current school or district vision statement?

Take a critical look at this statement. Is it memorable? How does it inspire action? Does it put your community on the path to the future, or does it reinforce the status quo? How do you articulate your own vision to ignite change? If there's a gap between where you hope to go and what your vision calls for, it may be time for a community visioning process.

Consider the essential conditions for effective research and development (R&D) in schools developed by the American School of Bombay (see p. 132 for full description):

- Empowered leaders
- Engaged communities
- Intrinsic motivation
- Future connection (i.e., optimism)
- Skill capacity
- Resource capacity
- Design thinking competence
- Impact validity

How robust are these conditions in your community now? Which conditions are absent or in need of further development? Which condition offers the best starting point for strengthening innovation in your school or system?

How Will You Support Teachers as They Become 21st Century Educators?

To encourage teachers as change agents, consider how your school or district supports their professional learning. What do teachers identify as gaps in professional development? What's on their wish list for professional learning (for example, conducting action research in their own classrooms or taking a field trip to see a particular pedagogy in practice)? If you're not sure, considering using an online survey or focus group to find out.

Chances are, many of your teachers are already exploring some of the practices that have the potential to be game changers for students. Who are the innovators and early adopters in your district or building? If you're not sure, how could you find out? How might you learn more about the practices they are using to engage students? How might you encourage teachers to share their innovative practices? How could you enlist these innovators as peer leaders?

Teachers in your community may already be using professional learning networks and taking advantage of connected learning (such as edcamps and #edchats) to drive their own learning. How could school leaders model and encourage connected learning for teachers? If given the opportunity and resources to design their own professional development, what would your teachers imagine? How could school leaders put their ideas into action?

How Will You Amplify Student Voice?

How aware of students' concerns are the adults in your building or school system? How would your students answer that question? To gather data, consider holding a listening circle hosted by student facilitators. (Recognize that student facilitators may need training in how to lead inclusive conversations.) Borrow strategies from #stuvoice to find out this from students: *What can you tell me about school that teachers and administrators don't know?*

As a learning community (including students), consider taking on one or more of these design challenges:

- How might we involve students in professional development?
- How might we modify instruction to amplify student voice in the classroom?
- How might we increase student voice in assessment?

How Will You Engage Families as Partners in School Change?

Take another look at Table 6.1 on page 99 that describes six types of parent involvement described by Joyce Epstein (first column) and traditional school activities commonly associated with them (second column). How is your school community engaging parents for change (as in the examples listed in the third column)? Where do you see opportunities to reframe traditional parent activities as engagement for change? How will you communicate with parents about the goals for these new roles?

Consider creating a family-friendly certification for schools in your community, modeled on the example of Boston Public Schools. Creating the process and standards for such an award could be an engagement strategy in itself, especially if you invite families to collaborate in a design event.

Who Else Will Join You?

As we have heard, increasing partnerships between school and community can produce mutually beneficial results, but these relationships require outreach and good communication. Develop your action plan for building partnerships by doing these things:

- Learn from your existing community partners. How do they currently engage with your schools? What do they say are the challenges or barriers to partnering? What motivates them to engage?
- Think more expansively about potential partners in your community. Map your community assets to identify museums, libraries, other government agencies, businesses, faith communities, youth-serving organizations, colleges and universities, service groups, and any other organization that might have a shared commitment to improving education.
- Identify a point person (or team) for cultivating partnerships and defining clear roles for partner engagement. Designate an "interpreter" to help educators and partners communicate effectively.
- Expand your network by asking partners for their recommendations.

How Will You Address Challenges and Build Momentum?

Change is hard work. Be clear about your purpose and your goals before you head in a new direction.

- Communicate the outcomes you hope to achieve. How will you define *better?* What evidence will you gather?
- Be transparent. Share stories of success as well as setbacks with stakeholders.
- Celebrate small wins.

Learn from the R&D model at the American School of Bombay (page 132), and track the accelerators that are driving change in your community.

Anticipate the "yeah, buts" you are likely to hear from resisters and be ready to respond.

HOW WILL YOU SHARE YOUR STORY
ABOUT THE FUTURE OF LEARNING?

Be strategic about shaping and sharing your own story about how teaching and learning are changing—and why. As Silvia Tolisano reminds us, school leaders take on the role of lead storyteller for their community.

As part of your action plan, consider which platforms and tools you will use to share your story. Social media can be useful, as we've seen in earlier examples, but only if it connects you with the stakeholders you want to reach. Find out which tools have the greatest traction in your community and use them to meet your stakeholders where they are, whether that's Facebook, Instagram, Twitter, a school website, a school YouTube channel, or your personal blog (or a combination).

Think about how you will capture and share the three kinds of documentation that you have heard about:

- Documentation OF learning
- Documentation FOR learning
- Documentation AS learning

Recognizing that busy teachers and school leaders may not have time to capture and share these artifacts, think about enlisting storytelling partners. We heard how the Remake Learning Network partners with public media to engage in storytelling about new ways of learning. You also might enlist students as documentarians or team up with school communication experts to capture stories worth sharing. Engage your students as ambassadors and storytellers, as well, by developing a student speakers' bureau or engaging students to lead school tours for community groups.

As you've heard in countless examples, school transformation depends on leaders and stakeholders who are inclined to act. They may need to troubleshoot if they hit obstacles. They may have to overcome the tendency to "snap back" to traditional mode when challenges occur. Begin to put your vision for school change into effect by determining this:

WHAT'S YOUR NEXT STEP? AND WHO'S WITH YOU ON YOUR JOURNEY?

Epilogue

Just as I was finishing this book, the winners of a nationwide competition for break-the-mold public high schools were announced. Over the coming five years, 10 new or redesigned schools across the United States will be underwritten with $10 million each from the XQ Super School Project. This philanthropic effort to spark innovation in education is the brainchild of Laurene Powell Jobs, widow of Apple cofounder Steve Jobs.

Many aspects of this ambitious project are remarkable, including the willingness of Powell Jobs to double down when she saw the outpouring of bold ideas from communities across the country. The original plan to fund five schools turned into a commitment to underwrite 10. (Iowa BIG, described in detail in the previous chapters, was named a runner-up and will receive $1 million over the next five years.) The winning entries, a mix of district and public charter schools, were selected from a pool of nearly 700 initial applications, which were winnowed to 348 semifinalists who submitted more detailed proposals. That tells us something about the wealth of ideas waiting to be implemented to transform teaching and learning.

Here's what else we can learn from this project: the 10 Super Schools are going to be laboratories of community partnerships. Stakeholder engagement was built into the application process, which required that proposals come from teams. New schools will work with community partners in all kinds of ways. Furr High School in Houston, Texas, which until recently suffered from a low graduation rate and a high number of disciplinary problems, plans to have students work with experts on environmental restoration projects with the goal of turning the school into a green hub for the community. Students at Brooklyn Laboratory in New York will look to the region's artists, universities, and tech sector as charging stations for engaged learning. At Grand Rapids Public Museum High School in Michigan, thousands of museum artifacts will be the launching pad for inquiry into community projects, including one of the country's largest river restoration efforts. Several schools serve students in high-poverty communities where innovative learning opportunities have been scarce. In the coming years, we can expect to learn more from these demonstration sites about how partnerships can improve outcomes for students and communities.

Meanwhile, many of the also-rans hope to proceed with their plans even without philanthropic backing. They may have to scale back their ambitions to meet budget realities or seek other sources of support, but they aren't ready to walk away from their inspiring visions to improve education. One team that didn't get past the semifinalist round told me that the very process of working on the application increased stakeholder engagement. The opportunity to think big together about the future of teaching and learning generated energizing conversations that included students, parents, teachers, school leaders, academic experts, and community partners. It was as if stakeholders were just waiting for the invitation to roll up their sleeves and get to work together.

I hope that the ideas in this book will provide the same kind of invitation to connect and collaborate with diverse stakeholders in your community. The challenge of transforming yesterday's schools into the learning environments that today's students deserve is too big, too important for any of us to tackle alone.

Appendices

A. *All Together Now* Online Resources
B. *All Together Now* Reading Group Guide
C. Books and Media to Spark Community Conversations

Appendix A

All Together Now Online Resources

The following links, mentioned as resources in *All Together Now* (many of which are displayed in shortened URL in the text) are included here in the order that they appear in the book.

CHAPTER 1

Christensen Institute definition of blended learning: www .christenseninstitute.org/blended-learning-definitions-and-models/

Connected Learning Research Network: clrn.dmlhub.net/

Educator Innovator: www.educatorinnovator.org/

Deeper Learning: www.deeperlearning4all.org

d.school Institute of Design at Stanford University: dschool .stanford.edu/

Design Thinking for Educators: www.designthinkingforeducators. com/toolkit/

P21, the Partnership for 21st Century Learning: www.p21.Org

Flipped Learning Global Initiative: www.flglobal.org

6 Principles of Genius Hour on TeachThought: www.teachthought .com/learning/6-principles-of-genius-hour-in-the-classroom/

Educating for Global Competence (free download): www .asiasociety.org/files/book-globalcompetence.pdf

Global Education Conference Network: www.global
educationconference.com/

Maker tools and strategies from Gary Stager and Sylvia Martinez: www.iste.org/explore/articledetail?articleid=106

Maker Ed: www.makered.org

iNACOL working definition of personalized learning: http://
assets.documentcloud.org/documents/1311874/personalized-
learning-working-definition-fa112014.pdf

Buck Institute for Education, elements of high-quality project-
based learning: www.bie.org/about/what_pbl

CHAPTER 2

Remake Learning Playbook: www.remakelearning.org/playbook/

Iowa BIG's Back-to-School Project archive: www.iowatransformed
.com/

Shadow a Student Challenge: www.shadowastudent.org

CHAPTER 3

Did You Know? Shift Happens presentations and resources:
www.shifthappens.wikispaces.com

Most Likely to Succeed, information about hosting a film screening: www.mltsfilm.org/

A Project by EdLeader21Profile of a Graduate Toolkit: www
.profileofagraduate.org

CHAPTER 4

Edchats calendar: https://sites.google.com/site/twitter
educationchats/education-chat-calendar

CHAPTER 5

Student Voice: www.stuvoice.org

Student Bill of Rights: www.sturights.org

CHAPTER 7

Humans of Cedar Rapids: www.humansofcr.org/

CHAPTER 9

Wooranna Park Raison D'être: https://drive.google.com/file/d/0BzQmyGcBw8K5NmZWbmY4SnQ1cEE/view

Remake Learning Competencies: www.remakelearning.org/competencies/

Appendix B

All Together Now Reading Group Guide

The focus on stakeholder engagement makes this book well suited to read and discuss with others in your community or in a professional learning network (PLN) of teachers. Here are some questions to frame your reading group conversations and encourage you to consider next steps.

Chapter 1: Are you ready for disruption?

The opening chapter suggests that diverse stakeholders bring different experiences, expectations, and perspectives about school. Begin your shared reading experience by discussing how your own education has served your needs. Can you recall specific school experiences that built a foundation you continue to draw on as an adult? Did school ignite passions that continue to burn bright for you? Looking back, do you recognize gaps in your education that you have had to overcome to achieve your goals? How well prepared do you think today's K–12 students will be to tackle the challenges ahead of them?

Chapter 2: How will we engage the willing?

The three case studies in this chapter (Pittsburgh, Cedar Rapids, and Dallas) begin with different conversational catalysts that engaged community members in thinking together about the future of education. Can you imagine similar stories unfolding in your community? What might be the spark to get people thinking together creatively about education?

CHAPTER 3: HOW DO FORWARD-LOOKING SCHOOL LEADERS TAKE CHARGE OF CHANGE?

Leadership expert Scott McLeod suggests that few school leaders feel a sense of urgency about school change. Do you agree? If you have worked with leaders who do bring a sense of urgency to the work, how does that affect everyone else in the school? (For example, is it inspiring or perhaps unsettling?) Has your school or district generated a profile of a graduate (as recommended by EdLeader21 and illustrated by the Mount Vernon Mind)? If not, take time now to discuss what you hope your students will know and be able to do by the time they graduate. How might you adapt an approach such as the dual operating system used by the American School of Bombay to fit your context? What would you anticipate as advantages and challenges to introducing such an idea? What else would you want to know before moving forward?

CHAPTER 4: HOW WILL WE SUPPORT TEACHERS AS THEY BECOME 21ST CENTURY EDUCATORS?

This chapter cites research indicating most teachers do not think their voices are heard when it comes to making decisions about education. Compare your own experiences of how your school community either invites or discourages teacher voice. When you have had a voice in decision-making, how did that influence your willingness to try something new? This chapter describes examples of peer-to-peer professional learning, such as edcamps. If you have participated in these events, what were your takeaways from the experience? How might your school do more to *deprivatize* the act of teaching, as we heard about in the Pittsburgh example? What feels risky about opening the classroom doors?

CHAPTER 5: HOW WILL WE AMPLIFY STUDENT VOICE?

Brandon Busteed of the Gallup Organization argues that the drop in student engagement for each year students are in school "is our monumental, collective national failure." How would you rate the level of student engagement in your community? Is your assessment based on personal experience, hard data, or a combination? Would students reach the same conclusion? This chapter describes a number of practical ways to increase student voice in learning. Discuss these ideas. Which ones are you interested in prototyping in your classroom or community?

CHAPTER 6: HOW WILL WE ENGAGE FAMILIES AS PARTNERS IN SCHOOL CHANGE?

Michele Brooks, former assistant superintendent of family and student engagement for Boston Public Schools, describes how parental roles need to shift at different stages of a child's life so that young people can become independent and capable of advocating for themselves. You may notice that none of the roles she describes include *helicopter,* a popular term for parents who are overly involved in managing their children's lives (often well into adolescence). What do parents need to understand about the importance of these stages when it comes to preparing students for the future—whether in college, careers, or citizenship? How might you help parents appreciate the importance of stepping back and allowing students to take more responsibility? Later in the chapter, you heard about strategies to engage parents who have not traditionally been involved in their children's education. What is your school doing to open the doors between school and home?

CHAPTER 7: WHO ELSE WILL JOIN US?

This chapter describes several examples of school–community partnerships. How are the Iowa BIG model and other examples different from the way your school system has approached partnerships with community organizations in the past? Do you have a "litmus test" for partnership opportunities, as Troy Miller of Iowa BIG describes? For the Glocal Challenge, the city of Cambridge, Massachusetts, is clear about setting expectations—for both youth and city staffers who serve as mentors. If you are recruiting adults for a similar mentoring role, how do you help them overcome challenges in dealing with students or troubleshoot problems as they arise?

CHAPTER 8: HOW CAN WE ADDRESS CHALLENGES AND BUILD MOMENTUM?

This chapter encourages you to define *better* when it comes to results for students. What is the "end in mind" you are imagining for students in your community? How will you know whether change has been worth all the effort and disruption? This chapter recounts familiar excuses ("yeah, buts") and concerns ("what-ifs") that naturally arise with any change effort. Which ones resonate? How will you prepare to address stakeholders' honest concerns without halting or derailing change efforts?

CHAPTER 9: HOW WILL WE SHARE OUR STORY ABOUT THE FUTURE OF LEARNING?

Wooranna Park Primary School in Melbourne, Australia, communicates its engaging approach to teaching and learning in words and videos shared online (for example, with a detailed raison d'être). These go well beyond the typical mission statement published on school websites or brochures. Other schools use social media to share scenes of transformed teaching and learning. How might your school expand its use of storytelling (both digital and face-to-face) to communicate what's worth knowing about your approach? What would you hope to gain from telling your story?

CHAPTER 10: WHAT ARE YOUR NEXT STEPS?

At the end of this chapter, readers are prompted to consider these questions: What's your next step? Who's with you on your journey? Discuss your answers to those questions. How will you begin to shift from talking to doing?

Appendix C

Books and Media to Spark Community Conversations

The following titles were mentioned in *All Together Now* as resources that have been used for shared reading or viewing to provoke community conversations about school change.

The Abundant Community: Awakening the Power of Families and Neighborhoods, by John McKnight and Peter Block, challenges communities to look within and recognize assets that may be hiding in plain sight.

Creating Innovators: The Making of Young People Who Will Change the World, by Tony Wagner, explores the back stories of several young adults who have already made their mark as innovators.

The First 90 Days: Proven Strategies for Getting Up to Speed Faster and Smarter, by Michael Watkins, focuses on the challenges that leaders must face at times of transition. Although not written specifically for an education audience, the book addresses strategies that should resonate with school leaders in times of change.

The Global Achievement Gap: Why Even Our Best Schools Don't Teach the New Survival Skills Our Children Need—and What We Can Do About It, by Tony Wagner, summarizes the skills demanded by the 21st century economy and the role of citizens in a globally connected world.

Invent to Learn: Making, Tinkering, and Engineering in the Classroom, by Sylvia Martinez and Gary Stager, connects the dots between constructivist learning and the maker movement, with an accessible discussion of tools and technologies to support learning by making.

Make Just One Change: Teach Students to Ask Their Own Questions, by Dan Rothstein and Luz Santana, introduces a simple but powerful formula for igniting student voice through inquiry.

Making Hope Happen: Create the Future You Want for Yourself and Others, by Shane Lopez, offers a psychologist's insights about the power of hope to fuel dreams and build resiliency.

A More Beautiful Question: The Power of Inquiry to Spark Breakthrough Ideas, by Warren Berger, celebrates the power of questioning as a foundation of problem solving and suggests strategies to keep genuine inquiry from "falling off a cliff" as students make their way through school.

Most Likely to Succeed: Preparing Our Kids for the Innovation Era, by Tony Wagner and Ted Dintersmith, accompanies the film by the same title (www.mltsfilm.org), which gives a close-up look at teaching and learning inside High Tech High in San Diego, California. Many communities have combined a screening with a panel discussion to provoke conversations about the future of school.

The Power of Vulnerability (www.ted.com/talks/brene_brown_on_vulnerability) is a TED talk by Brené Brown, a researcher who studies vulnerability, empathy, and shame. She shifts her focus from the academic to the personal in this popular talk.

The Third Teacher: 79 Ways You Can Use Design to Transform Teaching and Learning, a collaboration by three design forms (Cannon Design, Bruce Mau Design, and VS Furniture), explores the links between learning and built environment, offering case studies and visuals to inspire new visions.

References

Alexander, D., & Lewis, L. (2014). *Condition of America's public school facilities: 2012–13* (NCES 2014–022). U.S. Department of Education. Washington, DC: National Center for Education Statistics. Retrieved from http://nces.ed.gov/pubsearch

American Institutes for Research. (2016). *Does deeper learning improve student outcomes? Results from the Study of Deeper Learning: Opportunities and outcomes.* Washington, DC: Author. Retrieved from http://www.air.org/sites/default/files/Deeper-Learning-Summary-Updated-August-2016.pdf

Barth, R. S. (1997, March 5). The leader as learner. *Education Week, 16*(23), 56. Retrieved from http://www.edweek.org/ew/articles/1997/03/05/23barth.h16.html

Behr, G. (n.d.). Remaking learning: How it got started. *Pittsburgh Today.* Retrieved from http://pittsburghtoday.org/special-reports/remaking-learning-how-it-got-started/

Berger, R., Rugen, L., & Woodfin, L. (2014). *Leaders of their own learning: Transforming schools through student-engaged assessment.* San Francisco, CA: Jossey-Bass.

Bergmann, J. (2014, Dec. 16). Flipped learning toolkit: Getting everyone on board. *Edutopia.* Retrieved from https://www.edutopia.org/blog/flipped-learning-getting-everybody-on-board-jon-bergmann

Block, J. (2015, April 15). Learning from students. *Edutopia.* Retrieved from https://www.edutopia.org/blog/learning-from-students-joshua-block

Bogle, R. (2013). *Voice of the teacher.* Washington, DC: American Architectural Foundation. Retrieved from http://www.archfoundation.org/2013/01/voice-of-the-teacher-2/

Boix Mansilla, V., & Jackson, A. (2011). *Educating for global competence: Preparing our youth to engage the world.* New York,

NY: Asia Society Partnership for Global Learning and the Council of Chief State School Officers. Retrieved from https://asiasociety.org/files/book-globalcompetence.pdf

Boss, S. (2015, Sept. 21). Back-to-school products designed by students for students. *Edutopia*. Retrieved from https://www.edutopia.org/blog/back-school-products-designed-students-students-suzie-boss

Boss, S. (2016a, Summer). Making school new. *Stanford Social Innovation Review*. Retrieved from https://ssir.org/articles/entry/making_school_new

Boss, S. (2016b, May 9). Engage parents as partners to close the digital divide. *Edutopia*. Retrieved from https://www.edutopia.org/blog/engage-parents-partners-close-digital-divide-suzie-boss

Boss, S. (2016c, Feb. 5). Student innovators take local action on global climate change. *Edutopia*. Retrieved from https://www.edutopia.org/blog/student-innovators-take-local-action-global-climate-challenge-suzie-boss

Brengard, A. (2015, April 12). Redefining tech, culture and curriculum at Katherine Smith Elementary. *EdSurge*. Retrieved from https://www.edsurge.com/news/2015–04–12-redefining-tech-culture-and-curriculum-at-katherine-smith-elementary

Brooks, M. (2016, Feb. 8). *Five lessons learned about district leadership and family engagement*. Harvard Family Research Project. Retrieved from http://www.hfrp.org/family-involvement/publications-resources/five-lessons-learned-about-district-leadership-for-family-engagement

Brophy, J. (2013). *Motivating students to learn*. New York, NY: Routledge.

Brown, C. (n.d.). *Patterns of innovation: Showcasing the nation's best in 21st century learning*. Washington, DC: Partnership for 21st Century Skills. Retrieved from http://www.p21.Org/storage/documents/exemplars/P21_Patterns_of_Innovation_Final.pdf

Business Innovation Factory. (2014). *Students design for education* [Video]. Retrieved from https://vimeo.com/125506237

Busteed, B. (2013, Jan. 7). The school cliff: Student engagement drops with each school year [Blog post]. Retrieved from http://www.gallup.com/opinion/gallup/170525/school-cliff-student-engagement-drops-school-year.aspx

Casap, J. (2015, June 26). PBL World Conference Keynote. Napa, CA. Retrieved from https://www.bie.org/object/video/pbl_world_2015_jaime_casap_keynote

Chesterfield County (VA) Public Schools. (2012). Comprehensive Plan. Retrieved from http://mychesterfieldschools.com/wp-content/uploads/DfE2020/ComprehensivePlan%20DesignforExcellence 2020.pdf

Constantino, S. (2016). *Engage every family: Five simple principles.* Thousand Oaks, CA: Corwin.

Cooper, K. (2014, April). Eliciting engagement in the high school classroom: A mixed-methods examination of teaching practices. *American Educational Research Journal, 51,* 363–402.

Darling-Hammond, L. (2010). *Evaluating teacher effectiveness: How teacher performance assessments can improve teaching.* Washington, DC: Center for American Progress. Retrieved from https://www.americanprogress.org/issues/education/report/2010/10/19/8502/evaluating-teacher-effectiveness/

Dickinson, A. C. (2013, March 20). Re-imagining the comprehensive high school. *Edutopia.* Retrieved from https://www.edutopia.org/blog/sammamish-1-comprehensive-high-school-adrienne-curtis

EdSurge Research. (2016). Grassroots professional development: Heading to the digital frontier to learn. *EdSurge.* Retrieved from https://www.edsurge.com/research/special-reports/state-of-edtech-2016/k12_edtech_trends/professional_development

Fletcher, A. (2014). *The guide to student voice: For students, teachers, administrators, advocates, and others.* Olympia, WA: SoundOut.

Fullan, M. (2007). *The new meaning of educational change* (4th ed.). New York, NY: Teachers College Press.

Fullan, M. (2011). *Choosing the wrong drivers for whole system reform.* East Melbourne, Victoria, Australia: Centre for Strategic Education. Retrieved from http://www.janhylen.se/wp-content/uploads/2011/08/Fullan-Wrong-Drivers-Paper.pdf

Fullan, M., & Donnelly, K. (2013). *Alive in the swamp: Assessing digital innovations in education.* London, England: Nesta.

Gallup and Operation HOPE. (2013). *2012 Gallup–HOPE Index.* New York, NY: Operation HOPE.

Gallup, Inc. (2015). *Gallup student poll scorecard, Fall 2015.* Retrieved from http://www.gallupstudentpoll.com/188036/2015-gallup-student-poll-overall-report.aspx

Heick, T. (2014, Sept. 28). 6 principles of genius hour in the classroom. *TeachThought.* Retrieved from http://www.teachthought.com/learning/6-principles-of-genius-hour-in-the-classroom/

Henderson, A., & Mapp, K. (2002). *A new wave of evidence: The impact of school, family, and community connections on student achievement.* Austin, TX: National Center for Family and Community Connections With Schools, Southwest Educational Development Laboratory. Retrieved from http://www.sedl.org/connections/resources/evidence.pdf

Hoffman, S. (2015). *Curiosity projects.* Mumbai, India: American School of Bombay.

IBM. (2012). Leading through connections: Insights from the global chief executive officer study. Somers, NY: IBM Global Business Services. Retrieved from http://www-935.ibm.com/services/multimedia/anz_ceo_study_2012.pdf

Ito, M., et al. (2009). *Hanging out, messing around, and geeking out: Kids living and learning with new media.* Cambridge, MA: The MIT Press. Retrieved from https://mitpress.mit.edu/sites/default/files/titles/free_download/9780262013369_Hanging_Out.pdf

Jeynes, W. (2005). *Parental involvement and student achievement: A meta-analysis.* Family Involvement Research Digests. Harvard Family Research Project. Retrieved from http://www.hfrp.org/publications-resources/browse-our-publications/parental-involvement-and-student-achievement-a-meta-analysis

Joyce, B., & Calhoun, E. (2012). *Realizing the promise of 21st century education: An owner's manual.* Thousand Oaks, CA: Corwin.

Kelley, T., & Kelley, D. (2013). *Creative confidence: Unleashing the creative potential within us all.* New York, NY: Crown Business.

Kirtman, L., & Fullan, M. (2016). *Leadership: Key competencies for whole-system change.* Bloomington, IN: Solution Tree Press.

Kuh, G. (2007, Winter). What student engagement data tell us about college readiness. *Peer Review, 9,* 1. Retrieved from https://www.aacu.org/publications-research/periodicals/what-student-engagement-data-tell-us-about-college-readiness

Larmer, J. (2016, June 20). Making the most of PBL professional development [Blog post]. Retrieved from http://www.bie.org/blog/making_the_most_of_pbl_professional_development

Larmer, J., Mergendoller, J., & Boss, S. (2015). *Setting the standard for project based learning: A proven approach to rigorous classroom instruction.* Alexandria, VA: ASCD.

Lehmann, C., & Chase, Z. (2015). *Building school 2.0: How to create the schools we need.* San Francisco, CA: Jossey-Bass.

Loudon County Public Schools. (2015). *One to the world*. Ashburn, VA: Author. Retrieved from http://www.lcps.org/cms/lib4/VA01000195/Centricity/Domain/17509/OneToTheWorld_KeyElements.pdf

Luthra, S., & Hoffman S. (2015). *R&D your school: How to start, grow, and sustain your school's innovation engine*. Mumbai, India: American School of Bombay.

Martinez, S., & Stager, G. (2013). *Invent to learn: Making, tinkering, and engineering in the classroom*. Torrance, CA: Constructing Modern Knowledge Press.

Moore, H. (2014, Oct. 16). Embodied learning labs bring abstract science to life [Blog post]. Retrieved from http://remakelearning.org/blog/2014/10/16/embodied-learning-labs-bring-abstract-science-to-life/

Monarth, H. (2014, March 11). The irresistible power of storytelling as a strategic business tool. *Harvard Business Review*. Retrieved from https://hbr.org/2014/03/the-irresistible-power-of-storytelling-as-a-strategic-business-tool

Moran, P. (2015, July 28). Insight and outsight: 8 strategies to catalyze district-wide learning. *Edutopia*. Retrieved from http://www.edutopia.org/blog/insight-outsight-catalyze-district-wide-learning-pam-moran

Murphy, M. (2016, Summer). The tug of war between change and resistance. *Educational Leadership, 73*(9), 66–70. Retrieved from http://www.educationalleadership-digital.com/educationalleadership/2016summer

National Center for Public Policy and Higher Education and SREB (Southern Regional Education Board). (2010). *Beyond the rhetoric: Improving college readiness through coherent state policy*. Authors. Retrieved from http://www.highereducation.org/reports/college_readiness/CollegeReadiness.pdf

Organization of Economic Cooperation and Development. (2015). *Students, computers and learning: Making the connection*. Paris, France: OECD. Retrieved from http://www.oecd-ilibrary.org/education/students-computers-and-learning_9789264239555-en;jsessionid=34jaoc5rixr83.x-oecd-live-03

OWP/P Architects, VS Furniture, & Bruce Mau Design. (2010). *The third teacher: 79 ways you can use design to transform teaching and learning*. New York, NY: Abrams.

Palmer, B. (2013, March 29). Including student voice. *Edutopia*. Retrieved from https://www.edutopia.org/blog/sammamish-2-including-student-voice-bill-palmer

Partnership for 21st Century Learning. (2015a). *Sammamish High School: 21st Century Learning Exemplar Program.* Washington, DC: Author. Retrieved from http://www.p21.Org/exemplar-program-case-studies/1677-case-study-sammamish-high-school

Partnership for 21st Century Learning. (2015b). *Tips and strategies for families: Parents' guide for 21st century learning and citizenship.* Washington, DC: P21 and National PTA. Retrieved from http://www.p21.Org/our-work/citizenship/1582-tips-and-strategies-for-families

Puentedura, R. (2012). The SAMR model: Six exemplars. Retrieved from http://www.hippasus.com/rrpweblog/archives/2012/08/14/SAMR_SixExemplars.pdf

Quaglia, R., & Corso, M. (2014). *Student voice: The instrument of change.* Thousand Oaks, CA: Corwin.

Quaglia Institute for Student Aspirations. (2011). *My voice national student report (grades 6–12), 2011.* Portland, ME: Author. Retrieved from http://quagliainstitute.org/dmsView/MyVoiceNationalStudentReport(Grades6–12)2011

Quaglia Institute for Student Aspirations. (2014). *My voice national student report (grades 6–12), 2014.* Portland, ME: Author. Retrieved from http://quagliainstitute.org/qisa/library/view.do?id=459

Reimers, F., Chopra, V., Chung, C., Higdon, J., & O'Donnell, E. (2016). *Empowering global citizens: A world course.* North Charleston, SC: CreateSpace.

Remake Learning. (2015). About Remake Learning competencies and working group process. *Remake Learning.* Retrieved from http://remakelearning.org/competencies/#methodology-awareness-building

Rentner, D., Kober, N., & Frizzell, M. (2016). *Listen to us: Teacher views and voices.* Washington, DC: Center on Education Policy. Retrieved from http://www.cep-dc.org/displayDocument.cfm?DocumentID=1456

Rogers, F. (n.d.). *The Fred Rogers Company.* Retrieved from http://www.fredrogers.org/professional/

Rothstein, D., & Santana, L. (2011). *Make just one change: Teach students to ask their own questions.* Cambridge, MA: Harvard University Press. Harvard Family Research Project. Retrieved from http://www.hfrp.org/family-involvement/publications-resources/design-thinking-catalyzing-family-engagement-to-support-student-learning

Rowland, A. (2016, April). *Design thinking: Catalyzing family engagement to support student learning.* Harvard Family Research Project. Retrieved from http://www.hfrp.org/publications-resources/browse-our-publications/design-thinking-catalyzing-family-engagement-to-support-student-learning

Sheninger, E. (2016). *Uncommon learning: Creating schools that work for kids.* Thousand Oaks, CA: Corwin.

Sinanis, T. (2015, Feb. 4). Student led PD [Blog post]. Retrieved from http://leadingmotivatedlearners.blogspot.com/2015/02/student-led-pd.html

Stiggins, R. (2007). Assessment through the student's eyes. *Educational Leadership, 64*(8), 22–26. Retrieved from http://www.ascd.org/publications/educational-leadership/may07/v0164/num08/Assessment-Through-the-Student's-Eyes.aspx

Tarte, J. (2015, July 22). Student partnership in professional development. *Edutopia.* Retrieved from http://www.edutopia.org/blog/student-partnership-in-professional-development-justin-tarte

Taylor, L., & Parsons, J. (2011). Improving student engagement. *Current Issues in Education, 14*(1). Retrieved from http://cie.asu.edu/

Tenkely, K. (2016, March 25). What is sacred in education? [Blog post]. Retrieved from https://dreamsofeducation.wordpress.com/2016/03/25/what-is-sacred-in-education/

TNTP (The New Teacher Project). (2015). *The mirage: Confronting the hard truth about our quest for teacher development.* Brooklyn, NY: Author. Retrieved from http://tntp.org/assets/documents/TNTP-Mirage_2015.pdf

Tolisano, S. (2015, Sept. 9). Social media FOR schools: Developing shareable content for schools [Blog post]. Retrieved from http://langwitches.org/blog/2015/09/09/social-media-for-schools-developing-shareable-content-for-schools/

Tolisano, S. (2016, Jan. 1). The 3 stages of documentation OF/FOR/AS learning [Blog post]. Retrieved from http://langwitches.org/blog/2016/01/01/the-3-stages-of-documentation-offoras-learning/

Tomaszewski, S. (2015). *STEAM implementation and theory of action.* Pittsburgh, PA: Pittsburgh Public Schools.

University of Alaska Southeast–Juneau, Master of Arts in Teaching. (2016, July 1). Final reflections Alaska Studies 600 [Blog post]. Retrieved from http://uasmat.org/student-posts/final-reflection-600/

U.S. Department of Education Office of Educational Technology. (2015). *Characteristics of future ready leadership: A research synthesis.* Washington, DC: Author. Retrieved from https://tech.ed.gov/files/2015/12/Characteristics-of-Future-Ready-Leadership.pdf

Wagner, T. (2010). *The global achievement gap: Why even our best schools don't teach the new survival skills our children need—and what we can do about it.* New York, NY: Basic Books.

Warrick, T. (2015). *21st century learning exemplar program: Katherine Smith Elementary case study.* Washington, DC: Partnership for 21st Century Learning. Retrieved from http://www.p21.Org/exemplar-program-case-studies/1623-case-study-katherine-smith-elementary-school

Witt, R., & Orvis, J. (2010). *A guide to becoming a school of the future.* Washington, DC: National Association of Independent Schools. Retrieved from https://www.nais.org/articles/documents/naiscoaschools.pdf.

Wolpert-Gawron, H. (2015, Feb. 24). Kids speak out on student engagement. *Edutopia.* Retrieved from https://www.edutopia.org/blog/student-engagement-stories-heather-wolpert-gawron

Zhao, Y. (2012). *World class learners: Educating creative and entrepreneurial students.* Thousand Oaks, CA: Corwin.

Zhao, Y. (2014). *Who's afraid of the big bad dragon? Why China has the best (and worst) education system in the world.* San Francisco, CA: Jossey-Bass.

Index

A SAGE Publishing Company

Helping educators make the greatest impact

CORWIN HAS ONE MISSION: to enhance education through intentional professional learning.

We build long-term relationships with our authors, educators, clients, and associations who partner with us to develop and continuously improve the best evidence-based practices that establish and support lifelong learning.